RICH
PONDS

The Complete Guide To Identifying Rich Industries To Invest In

ANURAG SUNDARKA

SPOTLIGHT
by notionpress.com

SPOTLIGHT

by **N** notionpress.com

No.8, 3rd Cross Street, CIT Colony,
Mylapore, Chennai,
Tamil Nadu – 600004

First Published by Notion Press 2020

ISBN 978-1-64805-707-6

Reviews

Portfolio construction is not an easy task, neither for the novice students of the financial markets nor for the seasoned professionals, or the entrepreneurs wishing to deploy capital.

Rich Ponds, by Anurag Sundarka, breaks down the process of studying industries and identifying the most promising among them in such a clear and consistent way that makes it very valuable to everyone involved in the investment process. Highly recommended.

– DimitriosNousias,CFA
CIO, Whitetip Investments

"An important aspect of the investment profession is understanding a business. Numbers and balance sheet provide a good perspective on the past, but understanding qualitative drivers of a business is crucial in evaluating the future potential of any business. This book is an impressive attempt at providing a structured framework of evaluating not only any business (and its competition) but also evaluating industries."

– Samit Vartak
Chief Investment Officer, SageOne Investments

First rule of investing is to know where to look for investments. *Rich Ponds* provides an interesting take on identifying these industries. Leveraging Industry Sheet of *Rich Ponds* can help us in getting up to speed faster.

– Rajeev Agrawal
Founder and Managing Partner, DoorDarshi Advisors

Anurag Sundarka's *Rich Ponds* is aptly named as fishing (investing) becomes much easier after the fisherman (investor) has identified a pond (industry) which has bountiful catch (value preposition). The book prepares us to identify industries, enjoying lion's share of profitability due to their positioning in the value chain. This is a much-needed precursor to identifying great businesses to invest for superior returns.

While the content in the book is relevant for investment professionals, the language is simple enough for beginners & students of finance. The Industry Sheet provided towards the end of the book is well tailored for a quick reference & ensures that the book has immense practical utility. It has all the ingredients to be part of the bookshelf of all the investment professionals & students of finance.

– Sorbh Gupta
Associate Fund Manager-Equities
Quantum Asset Management

This book is a great read for investment professionals involved in fund management, equity research, etc. Typically you see that people get lost in numbers and take investment decisions. However, they forget that numbers are a result of operations, on-ground conditions, market dynamics, etc., etc. This book is a great attempt to throw light on those aspects. Also it is very well structured with clear checklists of what all needs to be understood!!! A good read for anyone in the investing world!!

– Executive Director at a leading Private Equity Fund

Not all industries are created equal. Some are brutally competitive where very few companies can survive and make profits. In others, almost every player survives and thrives. Anurag Sundarka presents a wonderful framework using qualitative and quantitative factors to help analysts and investors understand industry dynamics better so as to make better decisions.

– VikasKasturi
Value Investor

As an entrepreneur, when I wanted to understand business model, processes, practices, industry evolution, risk patterns and growth potential data – I never had a book or a place where I could gather all this data at one go. I have spent a lot of time in searching for it at various places.

That way Anurag has compiled this book very effectively and efficiently. His analysis, interpretation, data points, business model, industry analysis are very effective and will be very helpful for aspiring entrepreneurs and current business owners also.

This book – *Rich Ponds* is a manual and a significant contribution to our business & start-up ecosystem. For an aspiring entrepreneur this book – *Rich Ponds* is a treasure and an absolute treasure.

– Sathish Kumar
Founder – Creating Wealth
Equity Fund Manager | Wealth Consultant | Author

Contents

Foreword

I have always been a proponent of the ideology that in the coming era it's your skill sets that will be the biggest distinguishing factor. The more you pursue skill development, the better positioned you are for a better tomorrow.

I know Anurag since 2015 as someone who has had a lot of appetite to understand how to grow businesses. Being unconventional has been a key differentiator for Anurag. I still recollect how Anurag took one of the biggest plunges of his career; after being admitted in one the top undergraduate colleges of the country he decided to cancel his admission on the premise that he could not waste his time learning theory which didn't work and that he wanted to understand the real world. He had the spark, curiosity and enthusiasm to learn practically even before he started learning.

Anurag has been a star performer at our academy, all throughout. At a very young age, Anurag started working at one of the most respected investment management family offices in Mumbai.

This book is a reflection of Anurag's journey from a "fresher" having no technical knowledge to a practising researcher. Although Anurag is working on a series of such ideas, let me tell you why he decided to write the book *Rich Ponds – The Complete Guide to Identifying Rich Industries to Invest In* first.

To quote two legends of the Investing world –

Philip Fischer (Pioneer of growth investing): "In evaluating a common stock, the management is 90 per cent, the industry is 9 per cent, and all other factors are 1 per cent."

Charlie Munger (Vice Chairman, Berkshire Hathaway): *"Fish where the fish are."*

In short, if you want to make money through investing, you need to invest in powerful businesses and the probability of you getting a powerful business increases tremendously if you are in the right sector/industry.

Although Michael Porter and Michael J. Mauboussin have written research and books on evaluating industry structure, what is still missing is a holistic framework which can first of all help a starter understand how to apply this in the Indian capital market, with Indian case studies/examples and a step by step approach of analysing industries to be able to conclude about an industry potential.

Anurag has worked diligently to remove every minor and major bottleneck that a beginner faces like data sources, data extraction, industry templates, industry terminologies, etc. The book assumes no prior knowledge of the business world and will teach everything from basics. The brilliant part is the final section of the book where Anurag has designed the Industry Sheets – an industry analysis template. All you need to do is plug in the data in the template and the majority of the industry analysis will be taken care of. The book will make your life simple.

Anurag in reality has gone through the pain of a beginner and understands how a lack of a complete analysis framework can easily de-motivate someone from the path of generating wealth. This obsession has made the book exhaustive, lucid and practical. This book will act as a great guide to investors, business analysts, freshers, graduates and college professors equally.

– PRATIK ARYA
Lead Trainer and co-founder,
Finnacle Shah Investment Academy

Acknowledgement

Writing this book and coming up with the research work associated with the book has been a long journey. A journey that has spanned over years and changed me personally and professionally in more ways than I can think of. But, there is no way it would have been possible for me to do this alone. At every step in the journey, I had someone whom I could look up to for inspiration, learn from their work, keep up the motivation and at the same time also ask for help. I am immensely grateful. I probably cannot express in words here about how much it means to me.

I have to start with Pratik Arya and Inder Kapoor. They are the ones who first introduced me to the wonderful world of investing and not just that, hand-held me in my initial days at each step for me to not lose motivation when things got overwhelming. However, they took care to not hold hands so strictly that I would not make mistakes and that is where I grew. Pratik Sir has been my teacher, mentor and now a friend on whom I can blindly rely to show me the mirror. I am eternally grateful.

Moving on, I would like to thank Mr. Rajeev Thakkar. He is the one who instilled in me the kind of discipline an investor needs to follow. Next, Mr. Saurabh Jain and Mr. Ajaya Jain and the entire team at Astute

Investments that have helped me grow professionally. It is during my time at Astute Investments that the research work about the book started taking very concrete shape. I will always be grateful.

Next in line, I am thankful to all the work done by all the past authors, researchers and bloggers in the field. In no way was it possible to come up with this book without your work. I am just building on the phenomenal work done in the past. In fact, many ideas that were previously introduced by these authors have been included in the book, and I am just making them more implementable. In fact, I am seeing the world, standing on the shoulders of giants. I am very grateful to them. To name a few – Michael Porter, Michael Mauboussin, Alex Osterwalder and team, Sanjay Bakshi and Ramdeo Agarwal. I am incredibly thankful for the contributions you have made and I intend to add another layer to it through my work with 'Industry Sheets' and 'Qualitatives'.

Also, I would like to extend my gratitude to the team at NotionPress. The problems that a first- time author faces are uniques and am glad to have found a publisher who walked the same with me. Would like to thank the entire team there - Naveen, Swetha, Vidhya and everyone else who has worked tirelessly to bring this book to life.

Lastly, before I finish, I cannot end without showing my gratitude towards my mom, papa and my sister Radhika. They are the ones who have stood with me through thick and thin. I also would like to thank my friends and my entire faculty at Delhi Public School without whom none of this would have been possible.

I am incredibly grateful to all of you and I shall always be.

– Anurag

Introduction

This book is first in the series of books on the '9-point business circuit' model, which has been developed over years of research and trial and error. The 9-point business circuit is for anyone who wishes to own, start or analyse a business.

The basic premise of the circuit is a 'model-based thinking', which can be universally applied to any kind of business, in any industry or economy. The circuit has been designed using models that help break down businesses and understand critical areas related to investing, both qualitatively and quantitatively. The critical areas include industry attractiveness, competitive advantage of companies, financial strength, management expertise and incentives.

9 - Point Business Circuit

The remaining points on the 9-Point Business Circuit are related to firm-specific factors.

Not all industries provide similar opportunities for profitability. Some industries provide better scenarios for sustained profitability than others. Similarly, not all businesses within an industry earn similar profitability. This difference could be due to differences in business model, competitive positioning, approach by the management, or a combination of these factors.

Each point in the '9-point business circuit' relates to an industry or a particular business within the industry or both. Applying the models of the circuit will help identify industries that are relatively more profitable and businesses within them that perform better than their counterparts. The models will also help identify the 'why' behind such outperformance. For those who wish to own or analyse any business, the '9-point circuit' is designed as a framework around which they can build their analysis, without being overwhelmed by the quantum of raw data presented.

Starting out in any industry or venturing into an idea requires concrete research to understand the variables of the business. Once a business is operational, one of the most difficult tasks is to detach oneself while reflecting upon the business and strategies for the future. The 9-point circuit helps achieve the same. It also helps understand the basic characteristics of the industry, its attractiveness and the key success factors for firms in the industry. Then it constantly provides the questions that will help one think objectively about the business.

The elements of the circuit are:

1. Value proposition: Value proposition helps understand the product-customer fit and the value created on delivery. This can relate to a specific industry, based on what value the industry creates, or a specific firm. Each firm can tweak the value proposition to create a source of differentiation. Each new idea that one wishes to start with should be understood based on the value it would create and the product-customer fit it would generate.

2. Business model: Business model refers to the way money is earned and spent and the manner in which activities are carried out to create value. Again, it can relate to a specific industry, the way a particular business is carried out in industry, or a particular firm. Business models evolve over time; they are

generally a result of a series of small decisions over time, rather than one conscious decision. Some firms can deviate from the basic model and do things differently to create a source of differentiation.

3. Broad industry analysis: This stage relates to the industry level only and it helps understand the attractiveness of the industry. This elaborates aspects such as value chain, risks, demand-supply scenario, pricing power and competition within the industry.

4. Evolution of the industry: The evolution of the industry and various businesses in the industry help identify the key variables that impact the industry and establish 'precedence' regarding how firms have generally succeeded in the industry.

5. Trends and practices in the industry: The general trends witnessed in the industry help understand the possible changes and shifts the industry is going through. It also helps understand the common practices in the industry. With this understanding, one can challenge status quo for potential differentiation. This relates to the industry level only.

6. Risks and growth potential: These relate to both the industry-specific and company-related risks. The risks and growth potential of any industry apply to most businesses within it. Also, as companies are differently placed with different capabilities, they have specific risks and growth potential.

7. Competitive positioning: Within any industry, some firms are placed at an advantage to others. This competitive positioning is a cumulative result of smaller decisions regarding differentiation over time. Competitive positioning is at a firm-specific level only and not at the industry level.

8. Accounting story: The numbers of a business say a lot about the business—such as its quality, the people, and the changes, provided the right questions are asked. This stage helps understand the business quantitatively.

9. People: The people who run the business are the most important aspects of the circuit. They influence all the previous levels of the circuit. Understanding the vision, motivation and the ability of the management who are running the firm are critical aspects.

This stage is applied to each business separately and can be the reason for differences in the performance of otherwise identical businesses. This stage of analysis is not directly applicable to those who are running their own business.

First in the series, this book mainly focusses on understanding the attractiveness of any given industry. The book focusses on industry-level value proposition, followed by a broad industry analysis. Trends and practices in the industry, evolution of the industry, and industry-related risks and growth potential are then discussed to know more about the industry.

This book facilitates decision-making regarding attractive industries or what we call 'rich ponds' (potential fishing grounds) to find or start businesses with sustained above-average profitability. This book serves as a ready reckoner for analysts as well as investors who are on the constant look for great businesses and rich industries to invest in. It will help them systematically look for industries that have the fundamentals to raise healthy companies in them.

This book can also be used by entrepreneurs and business managers who actually carry out the business (whom we call practitioners) to analyse their ideas, the business and the industry in which they operate.

It will provide them a list of all the important questions to ask. The 'industry sheet' will help them identify the health of the industry. It will also help the analysts, investors and practitioners analyse and keep track of all the changes that could arise in any industry.

In this book, the spotlight is on the following elements of the circuit: value proposition, broad industry analysis, trends and practices in the industry, evolution of the industry and risks and growth potential of the industry.

The other elements of the circuit will be discussed in detail in the forthcoming books.

Value Proposition

Value proposition refers to the gains that a company's products and services create or the pains they relieve for a set of customers, in exchange for which they expect to earn a profit. The company's product and service offering must match the adequate set of customers who are looking to relieve themselves of similar pain or have similar gain requirements.

To elaborate, there must be a product-customer fit or match i.e. you must sell the right product to the right set of customers. For example, if you want to sell a Kindle, you must find people who are active readers and not look at the mass market.

Each company alters its value proposition and tries to be stronger than others in the same industry. The one with the strongest value proposition gets bought by the customer. However, another important factor is perception of value, which is subjective across different customers. Some customers may perceive a proposition to be very valuable whereas others may not even consider that proposition, depending on their pains and desired gains.

While designing the value proposition, the challenge is in getting the right match between the products and customers (product-customer fit). For example, while designing a car to be sold in the hinterlands of a country, one must take into consideration the needs of the customers. A luxury car may not be as effective as a tough car with a high fuel economy and an ability to ride on rough roads.

Value proposition can exist at the industry level as well as the business unit level. When comparing at the industry level, the value proposition must be compared to the value offered by substitute industries. For example, petrol car makers must compare their value proposition with that of diesel and gasoline car makers. Tea sellers should compare their proposition with coffee sellers. They should understand what gains are being created or what pains are being relieved. This will help sellers identify the buyers for their products and also make changes to the products to attract more buyers.

At the business unit level, firms are fighting among themselves on who would create the strongest value proposition. At the business unit level, firms must compare themselves and their offerings to those of other firms within the same industry as well as firms in substitute product industries. Substitute products are those that can be used in place of another. The firm can then decide which customer to focus on, which customer not to focus on, and how it should alter its products and services to better match the customer's gains and pains. There are two approaches to establish a value proposition with a good product-customer fit. The first approach is having products designed and then finding customers whose pains are relieved and customers who are looking for similar gains. The second approach is selecting a set of customers whom the business wants to service and then designing products and services that create value for them.

#Customers for Products

The first approach is a 'customers for products' approach. Here, the customers adapt to the value/features offered by the product. However, it is not so easy.

Making a good product or service is a monumental effort. But finding the customers who have similar pains and gains requirement as offered by the product is even more difficult. At times, despite the product being a great product, there may be no customers who are looking for the value offered by the product. Also, the effort magnifies, as often the people developing the product get attached to it and their biases make it difficult for them to see the product-customer fit objectively.

Despite the difficulties, there have been quite a few companies who have followed this approach and have found success. There are only two ways for this approach to work. Firstly, design a product so great that people forget their pains and gains and adapt to the value proposition offered by the product. This is a typical case of people adapting to products rather than the product adapting to people. Secondly, the product designed finds a customer whose needs exactly match the proposition offered by the product. However, the probability of this happening is very narrow.

When Steve Jobs said, "People hardly know what they want, until you show them," he was referring to building such a great product that people adapt their expectations to match what the product offers. Almost all businesses around scientific innovations and discoveries bet on customers adapting to their products rather than vice versa. However, such businesses are very rare and, to understand them, the technical aspects of the product need more attention than the economic aspects of the business. Such analysis is beyond the scope of this book.

#Products for Customers

It is relatively easier to study, predict and identify the needs of customers. Then one can design products that satisfy the pains and gains of the customers. Even companies that initially use the first approach eventually move to the second approach, which is designing products for its existing customers. For instance, many third-party logistics companies started providing financing solutions to their clients when they saw that their clients were looking for financing solutions for their inventory. Whether this is the approach that companies begin with or eventually arrive at, this is the approach that is used for our analysis.

To understand the value proposition of any industry or firm, each customer segment should be identified, for each of its products and service offerings.

There are multiple ways to divide the market into customer segments. They can be identified on the basis of any of the following five questions.

Who? Customers can be segmented based on who they are i.e. their identity, consumption patterns, tastes and preferences, which may vary based on origin. For example, some segment of the society or people of a certain country may show a similar buying behaviour.

Where? Segmentation is possible based on the geographical location from where the product is to be bought, sold or consumed. For example, consumers in northern India buy more diamonds compared to those in southern India, who mostly buy gold.

What? Segmentation can be done based on what people want or expect from a business. For example, some people go to the supermarket to buy grocery, while others go to the supermarket for dairy products or bakery products.

Why? Customers can be segmented based on why they wish to buy a product or service. The motivation can be the pains that will be relieved or the gains that would be created. For example, someone may buy a car for the purpose of transportation, whereas someone else may buy it for social status. Some people buy jewellery for consumption while others may buy it as an investment.

How? How the product would be used determines the segments in the market. The needs of someone who wants a laptop for gaming would be different from someone who requires it for basic MS office use.

The needs of those who use it daily would be different from those who use the laptop once in a while.

CUSTOMER SEGMENTATION OF INDIAN AGROCHEMICAL INDUSTRY

An in-depth look into how an Industry's customers can be segmented

The entire market for agrochemicals in India can be segmented based on the factors shown below. Each segment will behave differently from each other and will have a different customer profile.

The product and services should be designed differently for each segment. As a result, different firms in the industry can choose to target one or a few of these segments. Targeting each segment requires significant management bandwidth.

THREE BASIS OF SEGMENTATION

WHO	WHERE	WHAT
Crop type: creals and grains, oils and pulses, fruits and vegetables	Geography-wise: Northern India, Southern India, Western India, Eastern India, Central India	Agrochem type: fertilizers, herbicides, insecticides, pesticides, genetically modified seeds

Each customer segment is identified by a combination of all the different bases of segmentation. For example, cereal growers in Northern India looking for herbicides is a segment. Changing even one basis changes the segment.

Cereal growers in Western India looking for herbicides will form another segment. Also, the level of detailing for each basis depends on the scope of analysis. For example, each individual state for segmentation can also be used in place of regions for geography.

#Value Proposition Design

To understand the value proposition of the business and the product-customer fit, the products and customers need to be understood separately and then together, to understand whether the gains and pains are relieved or not, for the corresponding customer segments.

In the book *Value Proposition Design,* written by Alex Osterwalder, Yvette Pigneur, Greg Bernarda and Alan Smith, the authors propose a value proposition canvas. They say, "The value proposition canvas has two sides. With the customer profile, you clarify your customer understanding. With the value map, you describe how you intend to create value for the customer. You achieve fit between the two when one meets the other."

The value proposition model (in the book) focusses on products and services, the way they create gains and relieve pains, and the customer profile for each customer segment. The customer profile here would refer to all the gains that the customer wishes to create and the pains and risks that he wishes to relieve himself of, upon consumption of the product or the service.

This model should be applied for each product and service of the firm or industry and for each customer segment to understand what value is being created and how it is being created.

Value Proposition Model

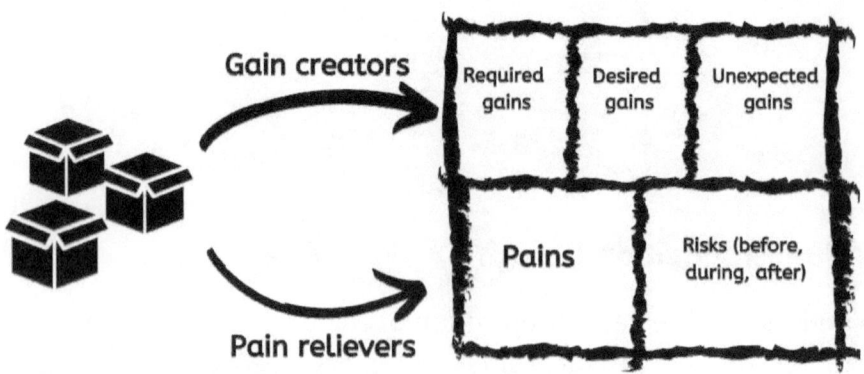

For those planning to launch a new product or service, all potential customer groups must be listed and then segmented based on the five questions mentioned earlier. A combination of the segmentation factors (who, what, how, why and where) can be used for an even more specific customer segmentation. The customer profile of each segment should be created and then the product or service that is being proposed should be altered to meet the needs and expectations of the customer segments selected out of all the potential customer segments initially identified.

Once the product creates the same gains and relieves same pains as desired by the customers, the product-customer fit would be achieved, and the product idea would find a market for it. If the product-customer fit is not achieved, the product will not find a market for itself.

For those analysing existing businesses or products, a slightly different approach is needed. As the sellers are already selling the products, they do have a product-customer fit. The objective here is to evaluate how strong the fit is and see if anything could be changed to increase the strength. Here again, based on the products and services sold, all potential customer segments must be identified. Each segment is then profiled and the best match for the products is identified. This is then compared to the segments being served by the business to identify if the correct segments are being served. Then the changes that could be made to the products to cater to other potential segments are identified. These changes would help the business serve more customers, identify growth avenues and also make the product-customer fit stronger. For example, when quick service restaurants (QSRs) such as McDonald's, Burger King and Pizza Hut came to India, they were selling pizza, burgers and fries. So many analysts anticipated these QSRs to shift to a menu based on Indian tastes and also offer a full-meal menu. This would open a bigger market for QSRs in India, analysts believed. And this did happen. Changes made to the product made the product-customer fit a much stronger one. This is the kind of mindset that analysts need to adopt when analysing a value proposition.

#Customer Profile

The first step after identifying the potential customer segments is to create each customer segment's profile. Creating a customer profile requires the investor to wear many hats. Firstly, he needs to be a researcher who collects facts about the customer's pains, gains and risks, through both primary and secondary research. He also needs to be an observer, who gets the facts based on the observation he has made while conducting his research. In some cases, the analyst may also have to wear the hat of a scientist, who, through his observation, drafts a thesis and then validates it through active research and experiment. The analyst must also wear the hat of detective. This is primarily because sometimes customers are not aware of all the pains that they want to be relieved of or all the gains they want.

The process of customer profiling is largely open-ended and subjective to the analyst, but the underlying principle remains the same. *Get as close to the customers and the buying process as possible.*

Some of the effective techniques to understand the customer better:

- Questionnaires

- Phone interview of the customers

- Phone interview of the middlemen

- Paid market research

- Online surveys of the past

- Videos on lives of potential customer segments

- Physical presence at point of sales.

- Physical presence at point of utilisation of product

SAMPLE QUESTIONNAIRE FOR AGROCHEMICAL RETAILERS

Q How does the customer buy the product? What are the variables they considers while buying?

Q What are the benefits and the major costs that the buyer perceives while buying agrochemicals?

Q How are the buyers educated or trained? How do they receive information about the products?

Q Do the customers buy mainly branded products or from unorganized players? Why?

Q Is there any community pressure while making a purchase decision?

Q Are the buyers confident about the use of agrochemicals? How much certainty do they have about the outcome after use?

Q Is the required agrochemical adequately available?

Q What are the payment terms for purchase by customers? Do they pay on time?

These, along with other creative methods, can be used to collect data to draft the customer profile. Insights related to customer psychology should also be incorporated in the customer profile.

The different elements of customer profile are discussed going forward. These would include gains, pains, risks and severity of each aspect. These would together form the customer profile. The gains required help understand the benefits that the customer is trying to achieve by consuming the product or service. The pains to be relieved relate to the discomfort that the customer is looking to get rid of upon consumption. The risks refer to the risks that he is trying to reduce. Each of these factors vary in the severity with which it affects the customer. Together they help create a profile for the customer, helping understand what the customer wants, what he wants to get rid of and what factors influence the purchase decision. These are discussed in detail going forward.

#Gains

Gains refer to what the customers wish to accomplish. It is the way in which customers wish to benefit from consumption of a product or service. Gains and pain relievers are the fundamental units that together create value for the customers. More the gains created, higher is the value created by the product. Gains can be created in two ways. Firstly, through cost savings and secondly, through enhancing the functional, social or psychological utility of the product.

For example, when a person buys a smartphone, it creates multiple gains for them. The customer can make a call, send messages, set alerts, listen to music, be connected on social media, and update social status. However, the priority of usage may vary depending on the customer segment being catered to. Also, some gains are functional in nature, whereas others are social or psychological in nature. Here is another example. When one signs up for a family vacation, the gains created are exploring new places, meeting new people, relaxing away from work, spending time with family, gathering new experiences, and trying out new cuisine.

Gains can be further divided into three levels.

#Types of Gains

1. Required gains: These are the basic gains that a customer requires. They are mandatory, without which the solution does not work and value is not created. For example, controlling room temperature when using an air-conditioner, making calls when using a smartphone, and mobility when using a car. These gains are fundamental to the product; the product can seldom exist without satisfying these gains. All successful products must fulfil these gains. Analysts need to pay attention to these gains as different customer segments have different required gains for the same product or service. This allows them to identify the segments that should be served and those that can be avoided. For instance, when dining out, great ambience may be a required gain by some; but it may only be a 'good-to-have' factor for others. The second segment of customers may have 'children's play area' as a must. Another segment may want a restaurant that serves vegetarian food only. These customer segments would have preferences that overlap with each other but each segment has a different required gain. That is why a detailed customer profiling is very important.

2. Desired gains: These gains are not basic or fundamental to the product but are 'desired' by the customer. Customers would want to have it if they could. For example, power efficiency and silence in an air-conditioner, beautiful design in a smartphone, and low maintenance and fuel economy in a car. These gains allow the product to demand a premium. Businesses with such products gain recognition over time and become strong businesses with sustained profitability.

3. Unexpected gains: Some gains are such that the customers do not expect them. In many cases, they do not even know that these gains can be created by the product or service. They are positively surprised when they come to know about these

unexpected gains. Often, the customers are not even aware of these gains till they start consuming the product or service. It is these gains that create customer delight.

For example, the experience that Starbucks creates in terms of service and ambience can be unexpected gains for any first-time visitor. Walking into an experience centre of Fab India, an Indian lifestyle company, can create a unique feeling in customers. The customisation service that it offers can leave customers positively surprised. It is businesses with such products that create unexpected gains. They win loyal customers and, over time, they go on to become great businesses.

Gains Required by the Customers of Agrochemical Industry - Pesticides Segment

REQUIRED GAINS	• Meet adequate requirements of the crops that farmer grows (basic crop protection) • Environment-friendly • Application of product permitted by the government • Usage guidance provided • Farmer's health should not be harmed on sustained usage
EXPECTED GAINS	• Awareness, consultancy and guidance • Reduced entry barriers - no special equipment should be required for application of the company's products • Environment-friendly for entire community • Focus on farmer's learning curve • Branded products for performance assurance • Community level accepted product to reduce social pressure
UNEXPECTED GAINS	• Low wastage application methods (formulations and equipments) • Promised or more-than-expected yield • Ease in credit facilities. Farmers only able to pay as per crop production in the given year • Give a higher sense of security i.e reduced doubt that crops could be destroyed by pests despite usage

#Types of Gains

Gains can also be broken down based on the nature and manner in which they create utility.

1. Functional gains: The customer tries to complete a particular task and the product allows them to do so. For example, a person uses a car for a functional gain—to go from point A to point B. The function of the car is to move from one place to another. Similarly, a pen that writes provides a functional gain. The stereo system in a car lets a person listen to music. This too is a functional gain.

All levels of gains can be functional in nature based on the manner in which they create value. Any gain, at any level, that enhances promptness, accessibility or easy reach to the value proposition is functional in nature.

2. Social gains: Humans are social beings with a desire to belong. This desire is described as a fundamental human motivation—a core factor that drives everything we as humans do. Creating a sense of belonging, whether with co-workers, friends or even online connections, is essential for our psychological wellbeing. Social proof acts as a fundamental building block to achieve this sense of belonging.[1]

Some gains delivered by the product or service create social proof and give the customer a sense of belonging to society. This can be in the form of social acceptance or social status, which leads to an enhanced perception in society. For example, apart from offering good performance, premium cars create a social status. Expensive watches and jewellery too create a positive social status. To some customers, this social gain is an important factor when a purchase decision is being

---

[1]   https://www.entrepreneur.com/article/317725

made. Creation of such gains creates a tremendous loyalty towards the product and allows the brand to command a higher price.

3. Psychological gains: When people make choices, they do not always do so objectively. The subjectivity in each decision is heavily influenced by the person's psychological preferences. These preferences are created over time, based on past experiences with the product.

Products create gains that are personal and psychological in nature and influence the preferences of the customers. For example, a restaurant's ambience, the designs offered by a clothing brand, and the sensory experience while using a particular perfume are gains that are psychological in nature and they impact the customers' preferences towards that product or company.

These gains are different from social gains. Social gains are approved by the society in totality; one person cannot alter what is 'accepted'. Whereas in psychological gains, the gains are very much personal and approved by the consumer. Products with such gains create immense attachment and customer loyalty.

4. Cost savings: The cost of consumption is the price paid for utilising the value created by the product. An increased cost of consumption is something that reduces the strength of the entire value proposition. Some products do not particularly focus on enhancing the gains created or the pains relieved, but they focus on reducing the cost of consumption. Thus, they pitch themselves to be of higher value than their substitutes or similar products. In the process of reducing cost, the product may let go of some gain creators—the ones that are low on priority for the customers. For instance, budget airline companies across the globe have cut out frills like food and provide cheaper fares.

Cost savings are not about financial savings alone. They could also be in the form of effort savings and time savings. Convenience products such as online bill payments and food ordering have found a huge market for themselves as they save a lot of time and effort for the customers. All these enhance the value for the customer and act as gain creators.

#Pains

Pains are obstacles, inconveniences or sources of dissatisfaction for the customers. The customer is seeking to get relieved of these pains. Pain is anything that is disliked by the customer. He or she cannot afford to ignore it and wishes to get relief from it.

Products that relieve the customers of their pains add value to the offering and strengthen the product-customer fit. If the pains of the customers are left unanswered or unattended to, the pains act as 'value destroyers' of the product and the business.

Customer pains can be before, during or after the process of trying to get a job done. Each dissatisfaction and dislike of the customers, through the entire process, should be identified, as each is a potential pain point that can be relieved.

Why is there a reference to relieving pain and not removing it? This is because pain removal is an illusion. It is not possible in reality. Trying to relieve one pain creates another. If we try to create the most perfect product, the cost in itself would become a pain. The idea is to relieve pains that are more severe, even if they create a few less severe pains.

Pain points come in all shapes and sizes. Products that have a hard-to-navigate service channel can be a point of pain. For instance, a website with an interface that is difficult to navigate is a pain point for customers. Products that have a high delivery charge or a customer service that is not very responsive can also be a pain point. Lack of clarity in prices, lack of transparency in the materials uses, or a sense of being overcharged when buying a product or service are all customer pain points. Some products may not be socially acceptable or the utilisation of the product may create a psychological dissatisfaction. For instance, consumption of alcohol and cigarettes is something looked down upon socially. Thus, it creates a pain for the customer.

No doubt customer pains are a challenge. But they are also opportunities for businesses to tweak the product-customer fit and create a source of differentiation over competitors or substitute industries.

Customer pains can be of different types, very much similar to the categories of gains.

1. Functional pains: These are pain points that occur during the application of the product and are related to the function or performance of the product.

    Pains that are functional in nature can be classified into four major types.

    – Financial pain points: The customer is spending too much money on the current service provider or product and wants to reduce the spend.

    – Productivity pain points: The customer is wasting too much time using the current service provider or product or wants to use time more efficiently.

    – Process pain points: The customer wishes the process behind the various tasks performed is improved; i.e. made stronger and more effective.

    – Support pain points: The customer does not receive the support needed at critical stages of the customer journey or sales process.

2. Social pains: These are caused by events such as exclusion from social connections or activities, rejection or bullying. This is due to consumption of products that are not accepted in the

immediate surroundings of a customer and it creates pains that are social in nature.

In February 2014, a study titled 'Empathy for social exclusion involves the sensory – discriminative component of pain: a within-subject fMRI study' said, "Our data have shown that in conditions of social pain there is activation of an area traditionally associated with the sensory processing of physical pain, the posterior insular cortex." This shows the impact social pains can have on customers; they can act as huge value destroyers for the customers. Any product that is looked down upon by society in itself or through its application creates social pains.

For instance, poorly maintained automobiles that damage the environment are looked down upon in certain developed countries. Sportswear from inferior brands creates social pains for the customer.

Social pains in any customer segment is relative to the immediate surroundings of the customer. Something that creates social gains in some surroundings can create social pains in others, based on how the product is perceived. For instance, wearing a particular brand of watch may create social gains in some surroundings whereas create pains in other surroundings.

3. Psychological pains: Psychological pains are created due to beliefs, thoughts, feelings and behaviour that arise during the process of consumption of a product or service or completion of a task. Products or services that make the customer believe, think, feel or behave negatively create psychological pains. For example, if the customer does not like the colour or smell of a product, that can cause a psychological pain. If the customer does not like the buying process, it can cause a psychological pain. If the person selling the product is perceived to be very unfriendly and rude, this too can result in a psychological pain.

Psychological pains vary in their impact and intensity, from person to person. A complete understanding of human psychology and customer behaviour is required to keep track of psychological pains encountered by the customer during the purchase and consumption processes.

Pains of Customers that Need to Be Relieved for Agrochemical Industry - Pesticides Segment

BEFORE USE	• Lack of awareness about what product to buy • Inefficient selling by unorganised retailers • Sense of being cheated common among farmers • Improper information by retailers to sell more • High application equipment costs • Community pressure against excessive use of pesticides • Uncertainty about performance of product and return on investment - a huge psychological barrier
DURING USE	• Lack of knowledge about how to use the product and in what quantity • Improper safety equipment and high costs of safety equipment • Health hazards for the farmer due to chemical exposure • Wastage in application reduces efficiency and increases cost • Uncertainty about outcomes creates psychological barriers
AFTER USE	• Health effects for the entire community due to long term usage of chemicals • Soil health of the land on which crop is being produced • Inability to pay for the costs of pesticides if the crop is destroyed or a poor harvest is obtained

#Risks

All decisions are some sort of trade-offs between the costs and benefits of potential items that could have been chosen by the customer. Each decision brings with it certain risks and a feeling that one has perhaps made a wrong decision. The risk is directly in line with the amount of uncertainty about the future course of action from choosing any of the potential items.

Risk also arises during the process of getting a task done. Some risks affect the customers in their general course of life. Products or services that do not create any additional gain or relieve pain but reduce the risk in consumption create tremendous value with customers. The more severe the outcome of the risk could be, greater is the value created and greater is the ability of the business to demand a premium for it.

For example, insurance policies do not create any obvious gain or relieve any obvious pain. But they provide the customer certainty about the future and protection in case the risk materialises. Let us look at another example. As car accidents become more and more frequent, the safety features of the car become an important factor while making a purchase decision. Cars with airbags are instantly preferred as they reduce the impact in case of an accident. Products that reduce potential undesired outcomes have the ability to garner recognition in the market and demand a premium.

RISKS FACED BY AGROCHEMICAL BUYERS – PESTICIDES SEGMENT

FINANCIAL RISKS

Financial performance of investment in pesticides depends on the benefits received against cost of inputs by the farmers. There is a risk of high investment and low pay-off for farmers, which pushes many into debt.

SOCIAL RISKS

If a farmer chooses to use a pesticide that is not commonly used by the entire community, it has huge social implications for the farmer in case of failure and a poor yield using the product.

LACK OF KNOWLEDGE ABOUT HOW TO USE THE PRODUCT

Farmers are not completely trained for usage of pesticides and depend on retailers or field officers of companies for education. At times, they may end up overdosing or underdosing their crops and thus hurting produce.

ENVIRONMENTAL IMPACTS

Continued usage of pesticides harms the environment and soil health. Over the years, it may even make the land unsuitable for production. So, farmers need to keep a check on the environmental effects of pesticides.

COUNTERFEIT PRODUCTS

Farmers often get cheated by retailers as they are provided counterfeit products. This is a risk that farmers face while buying any pesticide.

PESTS GETTING USED TO THE PRODUCT

Over time, pests get used to a particular pesticide due to the evolutionary processes. What had worked in the past stops to work and farmers face pest attacks due to this and are exposed to this risk.

On each purchase and consumption of a product, farmers face this risk. Any company that can reduce these risks creates a huge value for the customer.

#Severity

All pains and gains are not equally important. Some pains may be more important and pressing (to be relieved) than others in a particular segment. Some pains may be less important or urgent in other customer segments. Also, different customer segments may be willing to pay different amounts for the same gain, as each gain is perceived differently. Hence, each pain, gain and risk needs to be prioritised based on it severity and relevance to the customer group.

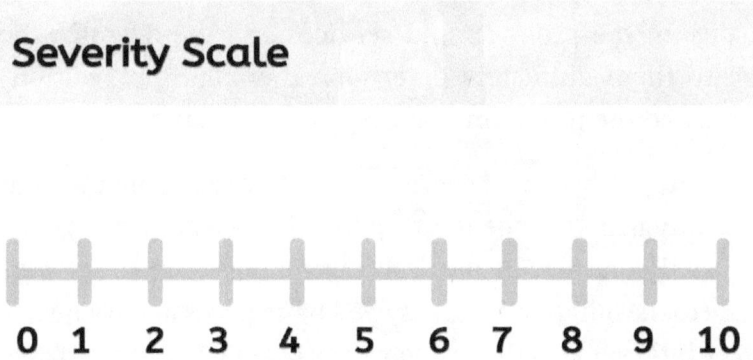

Severity Scale

0 1 2 3 4 5 6 7 8 9 10

Each pain and gain should be identified in terms of the severity with which it affects the customer. For instance, the performance of the car heater may not be as important in Western India as it is for the customers of northern India. The quality of the camera in a phone is more important to artists than others. When trying to understand the severity, the analyst needs to look into as much depth as possible, and talk facts and numbers. For example, when a customer says waiting in line was a waste of time, the analyst must ask the customer after how many minutes the wait began to feel like wasted time. Objectivity is essential in understanding the relative differences between the severity of various gains, pains and risks.

#Products and Services

For customers, the value is the benefits of the products and services of the firms. Once the customer has been segmented, each segment has been profiled, and different gains and pains have been mapped, the products and services need to be matched with the customer profiles, so that they create relevant value by generating relevant gains and addressing the correct pain points.

Products and services act as a 'store of value' for businesses, which are ultimately delivered through the purchase and consumption process. The quality of the products and services and the overall experience attached to them ultimately determine the value proposition of the businesses and the premium that they can command.

However, products and services do not create value by themselves. They must match the needs of appropriate customer segments. For example, an iPhone may be the best smartphone there is, but it is of very little value to the illiterate. Cars may be a basic necessity to some, but they are of very little value to the residents of a remote island or village, which has no roads or fuel supply. On the other hand, even a mediocre torch would be of great value for customers of a village with no electricity.

For existing businesses, products and services are pretty easy to identify. Each has to be understood based on how it solves the customer pains and gains. Businesses must understand their product in and out and then try to figure out if any changes could be made to the product to serve newer segments of customers (other than existing customers). Businesses can also try to serve existing customers better and demand a higher premium from them. They must look for substitutes that exist in the market and understand the manner in which they create value for customers.

Some offerings of these substitutes that are important to the customers may even be incorporated in the firm's products. All the propositions compete against each other and only the strongest proposition gets bought. The strongest proposition for each customer segment may vary but it is only the strongest proposition that each respective segment will buy.

For new businesses or existing businesses that are trying to design and launch a new product, the entire process involves a lot of trial and error and continuous testing. Once the customer profiling is done, the most lucrative set of customers that should be serviced are identified. The product is designed in such a way that the pains and gains that are high on the priority list are serviced immediately. The process involves developing a prototype, testing it with a small trial group, making changes as per the feedback, and then test marketing followed by the launch. Businesses must look for customer feedback and continuously monitor their experience and satisfaction. This must be done throughout the process and even after the launch for continuous improvements.

The features of the products and services can be segregated as pain relievers and gain creators. The features that relieve the customers of their pain is a pain reliever whereas those that create benefits for them are gain creators. For instance, an easy interface in a mobile application would be a pain reliever whereas the food home delivery service of that app would be a gain creator. It is essential that pain relievers and gain creators of the product are designed so as to suit the profile of the customers.

#Pain Relievers

Pain relievers include the features of the product or service that relieve the customer of the pains and the manner in which the pain is relieved. They focus on the 'what' and 'how' of the product and the process of its purchase and consumption. Pain relievers can be understood only if all the pains of the customers and the priority of the pains to be relieved are understood.

It is hard (or rare) for value propositions to cater to all the pains identified in the customer profile. So, products should initially focus on the most severe pains and then, over time, add features that cater to the other pains of the customer. The importance and relevance of the pain reliever depend on the severity of the pain. A pain reliever that releases a customer of a pain that is not very high on priority is not likely to create a lot of value for the customer.

PAIN RELIEVERS BY AGROCHEMICAL INDUSTRY

Field officers

Field officers go to the field and increase awareness about various products and how to use them. This helps the farmers stay up-to-date with the new offerings.

Community engagement events

Agrochemical companies organise farmer community engagement events. These events give social proof to the products and reduce community pressure in case of failure.

Safety equipment and knowledge

Companies often provide safety equipment to farmers at a lower price. They also provide information about their health safety. This is to reduce health hazards for farmers.

Favourable forms of application

Agrochemical companies try to make agrochemicals in such a form that application has the least wastage. For example, powders or drip application methods.

Brands and lab test approvals

Agrochemical companies try to build brands and share lab test reports to reduce uncertainty relating to underperformance in the farmer's minds.

How to differentiate

We see that not all pains are relieved by the current value propositions. New firms can come up with innovative solutions and create a stronger proposition. Examples of initiatives: Give free application instruments or innovative mechanism to allow credit flexibilty.

#Gain Creators

Just like pain relievers, gain creators too include the features of the product or service that create benefit for the customers and the manner in which the benefit is delivered. They too focus on the 'what' and 'how' of the product. The process of consumption and purchase also influence how the gain creators are delivered and perceived. Gain creators play a big role in determining the expectations of the customer. Their fulfilment will decide if the customer is delighted, merely satisfied, or not impacted by the consumption of the product.

All the gains required by a customer cannot be answered. Some gains are higher on priority and the corresponding gain creators are therefore higher in terms of premium. Companies should address the most important gains and create what is called a 'minimum viable product' and then add features to it with time. For instance, when purchasing a house, a minimum viable product is an apartment that is safe, built of good materials, has a neat design, and adequate parking. Other features such as fitness facilities, clubhouse and play areas may be added along the way, after the hygiene factors are taken care of.

In an attempt to create multiple gains or relieve multiple pains, the company may fall into the trap of doing too many things, at the same time. It may engage in many activities that have no direct impact on the customers of the company or their pains and gains. The company may even end up targeting the wrong set of customers with its products and services. The company officials, as well as the analysts, must be careful and try to identify such wasted efforts. These are not just a waste of time and effort per se, but they also take away energy, attention and resources from the value-creating activities.

GAIN CREATORS FOR AGROCHEMICAL INDUSTRY

LAB-TESTED CROP SOLUTIONS

Lab-tested solutions create more assurance in the minds of customers about what performance can be expected from the product.

GOVERNMENT-APPROVED PRODUCT

Not all agrochemicals can be used by the farmers. Only those that are approved by the government can be used. Unapproved products invite litigation risks.

RETAILER TRAINING

Retailers need to be trained to provide information to the buyers about usage. Besides usage guidance, they can also help in creating awareness.

HELPLINE

Companies need to establish a helpline so as to resolve specific farmer queries at different stages of the entire process.

STANDARD APPLICATION EQUIPMENTS

Some products require specialised application equipment, whereas others can use standard equipment. Standard application reduces entry barriers and creates gains for the customer.

Not all gains that are required can be created. Firms that can create more gains at a cheaper rate strengthen value proposition.

To sum up, to complete the value proposition model analysis, the products and services should be identified once the customer segmentation and profiling has been done. The features that create value should be identified and the way value is delivered should be articulated. These will form the pain relievers and gain creators. Then they should be ranked in order of importance based on the severity of each pain and gain to be addressed. However, this entire process assumes that customer profiling has been done properly. As the first step in both analysing existing products and creating new products is effective customer profiling, no analyst should rush during the step. When more and more time is spent on customer mapping, new insights will be gained, which will help strengthen the value proposition. Also, customers are continuously evolving and changing their requirements. Thus, the process of customer profiling and then accordingly adjusting the features of products and services remains a continuous one.

The features that create value should be identified and the way value is delivered should be articulated.

- *Take time to do the customer profiling. Do not rush this process.*
- *Customers keep changing. So, customer profiling and product tweaking is an ongoing process.*

While evaluating disruptions and their risks, the value proposition model is key to check if the disruptor would be successful or not. This helps compare and contrast the substitute industry and the original industry.

The industry that creates the most value will survive over the others. For instance, compare the traditional petroleum cars industry with the electronic vehicles industry. The model will provide an objective regarding the pains and gains created by both industries, how they are perceived by the customers, and which offers a stronger value proposition against the price paid. The one with the stronger proposition is the industry that will do better going forward.

Within industries, the value proposition model can be used to identify the businesses that are offering a stronger value proposition and replace the weaker ones going forward. This can be used to track any innovation within the industry to create more value for the customers. Thus, the value proposition model should be used at both the industry level and the business level.

Here are some examples and case studies of popular brands, which will help you gain more insights.

CUSTOMER SEGMENTATION FOR INDIAN RETAIL BANKING CUSTOMERS

WHO

- Individual
- Business owner
- Senior citizen
- NRI

WHAT

- Transactions
- Loans
- Insurance
- Investments
- Banking services

WHY

- Convenience
- Economic benefit (financial gain over convenience)

HOW

- Active banking user
- Not very active user

COMBINE ANY COMBINATION OF THE ABOVE SEGMENTATION FACTORS TO GET DISTINCT CUSTOMER SEGMENTS.

CUSTOMER PROFILE FOR RETAIL BANK

Individual segment

PAINS TO BE RELIEVED	GAINS TO BE CREATED
BEFORE BANKING • Complicated banking products, not understood by customers • Bank branches not available in proximity for customers • Minimum balance requirements for accounts • Lack of awareness about existence of products	**REQUIRED GAINS** • Safety of deposited money • Convenience, accessibility • Mobile accessibility for most services • Par risk adjusted return on investments
DURING BANKING • Lack of response from bank employees • Slow and lengthy processes • Hidden charges • Inefficient banking software, servers and poor internet connectivity, especially in remote branches • Long lines and heavy rush at branches	**EXPECTED GAINS** • Responsive customer service • Personalised product offerings • Processes to be quick • Fair economic benefit - low premiums and high interest returns • Loans with repayment schedules customised for business • Accessible business related services • Low transaction and service charges
AFTER BANKING • Unfair charges • Fear of fraud • Misconduct of account by someone else	**UNEXPECTED GAINS** • Easy, hassle-free loans • Personalised relationship manager • Favourable customer benefits of using the banks services - loyalty programs, discounts on various portals

PSU BANKS

Pain Relievers

- Dense branch networks
- No minimum balance requirements
- No unfair charges. Low charges for transactions and services

Gain Creators

- Dense branch networks (Especially in tier 3 and below) - Increases accessibility
- Secured by the government - high safety of money
- Preferential offerings for women and senior citizens
- Low transaction charges and other service charges
- Mobile applications available
- A few customer loyalty programms and partnerships -E.g. SBI- Yatra , SBI-Flipkart

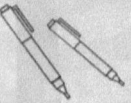

PRIVATE BANKS

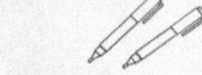

Pain Relievers

- Dense branch networks (mainly in tier 1, 2 and 3 areas)
- Prompt response from employees
- Awareness campaigns and customer relationship managers
- Less rush in branches
- Convenience: mobile and net banking

Gain Creators

- Mobile and net banking accessibility
- Relationship manager with responsive service
- Personalised product to suit needs
- Relatively quick processes as most documentation is in digital form
- Tailor-made loan repayments
- Easy business related services and innovation in services
- Many customer loyalty programms and partnerships

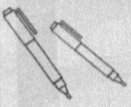

WHY ARE PEOPLE SWITCHING FROM PUBLIC BANKS TO PRIVATE BANKS?

On comparing the two value propositions, we conclude:
- PSUs were favoured mainly for two reasons - safety of capital and dense branch network.
- With private banks gaining size, they have also established trust regarding safety of capital, particularly with new-age customers.
- As they have gained scale, they have also widened the branch network, particularly in metros, tiers 1,2 and 3.
- Along with reducing the advantages of public banks, private banks offer ease and convenience in banking, personalised products, innovative solutions and quick services.

As a result, private sector banks have been able to attract a lot of customers from slow and lethargic public sector banks.

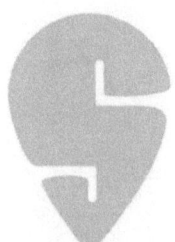

WHY DID SWIGGY WORK AND OTHERS FAILED?

Food tech companies across the globe were struggling in late 2013. This was when Swiggy came up in Bangalore and changed the industry. The difference was to build own logistics network rather than outsourcing it. Here is the customer's profile, which explains why own logistics network of Swiggy succeeded.

PAINS OF CUSTOMER	OLDER BUSINESS MODEL	SWIGGY MODEL	GAINS REQUIRED BY CUSTOMER	OLDER BUSINESS MODEL	SWIGGY MODEL
HEAVY DELIVERY CHARGES	✗	✓	FRESH FOOD DELIVERED	✓	✓
SLOW AND UNRELIABLE DELIVERY	✗	✓	MULTIPLE CUISINES TO CHOOSE FROM	✓	✓
LACK OF STANDARD DELIVERY ACROSS CITIES	✓	✓	SINGLE WINDOW FOOD AND DELIVERY ORDER	✗	✓
OVERCHARGED ON FOOD FOR DELIVERY	✓	✓	DISCOUNT OFFERS ON FOOD	✗	✓

*Pains and gains are in order of significance.

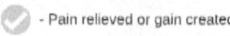

✓ - Pain relieved or gain created   ✗ - Pain not relieved or gain not created

Earlier food tech companies in India were pure marketplaces where they received orders and passed on to restaurants. Logistics was left either to the restaurant itself or was done by third party players. This would lead to the customer paying a high delivery fee and non- standardised delivery.

Swiggy, followed by Zomato are Indian startups which entered food delivery business in 2013 and 2015 respectively. They tied up with restaurants and give them orders that they had received. However, the difference was that they had built their own logistics network and did all the delivery themselves. This allowed them a pan India standardised food delivery. Also, they had extended a lot of discounts and deals that got the customer into the habit of ordering online food. The standard delivery mechanism and discount deals is what got swiggy and zomato to create a stronger value proposition for the customers.

WILL BYJU'S WORK IN INDIA?

Byju's is an online education app for Indian students and provides on-demand classes for the students of various subjects. The app has been well received by investors, and also has also given a proof of concept with the customers. The key question is whether it will be a success in India and students will actually switch or it would fade away over time.

CUSTOMER PROFILE

PAINS	GAINS REQUIRED
Expensive tuition classes	High quality result-oriented education for kids and for competitive exams
Lack of standard quality teaching and faculty	Quality mentorship
Big batches for students; inadequate attention	Personalised attention to each student
One-size-fits-all way of teaching	Enough practice for the subjects
Lack of flexibility in timing	Regular performance reviews
Travelling is an issue for remote areas	Personal connect with the teacher
Irregular and inefficient performance reviews	Trust on the teachers and their style of teaching

Once the customer profile is known, it has been established what the customer wants. This should then be comapred with what is being offered to the customer. The features of the product and service that reduce pain or create gain must be understood to understand the product - customer fit.

VALUE PROPOSTION

PAIN RELIVERS	GAIN CREATORS
Moderate costs (Neither too expensive, nor too cheap)	Quality courses, created and curated by experts
Standardised teaching practices	One on one attention given (Personalised chats and calls arranged)
Individual students, no batches	Performance based practice given
Personalised performance based practice given	Weekly and monthly performance reviews given
Complete flexibility in timing	Parent's can continuously keep a track of child's progress
Regular performance reviews	
Available over internet. No travel is needed	

CONCLUSION

It is seen that Byju's relieves the customer of almost all pains and creates most of the gains. However, Byju's is unable to create trust that it will produce results for students in a short period of time. However, over time, Byju's should be able to create the required trust as more and more people get used to its product.

Another hindrance for Byju's would be data charges. However, in India, with such cheap data, this is not a pain for customers. But if data prices rise, it can be dangerous for Byju's.

Besides these two factors, it is observed that Byju's has a good customer-product fit and shall do well going forward.

All new ideas and products must be checked in a similar manner under the 'value proposition map' to see if they have a strong customer-market fit or not. Only ideas that pass this will find a market for themselves.
'Customer profile' is the key.

Broad Industry Analysis: An Overview

Once the value proposition by the industry and its constituent players has been understood, more specifics about the industry's activities, players, risks and demand-supply scenario can be looked into. Further analysis is done to understand the industry size, stability, pricing power, disruptions and regulations. The profitability trends in the past for the industry is analysed and the future direction is sensed based on Michael Porter's five forces framework. These attempts together form the third point of the 9-point business circuit. *(More analysis on the second point, 'business model map', will be done in another book on firm-specific analysis.)*

This stage comprises a four-tiered analysis structure.

The first tier gives an understanding of the activities done in the industry, the constituents of the industry and other industries with which the given industry transacts, the profit pool within the sector, the major risks, and the demand-supply scenario. This stage gives a very macro-oriented view of the industry.

The second tier gets deeper into the composition of the industry and the behaviour of the various constituents. Here the total market size is identified along with the composition of the organised and unorganised market. How the market has evolved over time is also understood. The industry stability is studied based on the gaining and losing of market share by the top players. The pricing power of various industry participants is also analysed. Attention is given to the competitive life-cycle positioning of the constituents and the risk of disruptions. Government regulations for the industry, recent news related to the industry, and ongoing trends in the industry are also identified in the second tier.

The third tier focusses on identifying how Porter's five forces affect the industry and provides a list of questions that can help judge the strength of influence of each force. There is also an emphasis on identifying any changes in the forces and the industry structure going forward.

The fourth tier is much more quantitative. It focusses on profitability, its asset intensiveness and use of leverage i.e. debt by the top companies of the industry. At times, this step is affected by the company-specific decisions. But, by taking into consideration a large number of companies, a broader picture of the quantitative performance of the industry participants can be understood.

First Tier

#1 Value Chain Analysis

The value chain analysis framework was first described by Michael Porter in 1985, in his book *Competitive Advantage*. This book primarily focusses on analysis at the company-specific level. But, with time, the model has evolved into something that is used for analysis at the industry-specific level as well. At the company level, the model is used to identify activities that create a source of differentiation or cost saving with respect to competitors. The value chain represents generic internal activities that a firm engages in to transform inputs into outputs.

At the industry level, the value chain is used to understand the way of doing business in the industry. Company-specific activities are eliminated and the entire process of value creation and delivery is understood.

Value chain analysis at the industry level allows the process flow to be mapped. It shows the major activities carried out by a majority of the firms in the industry. It shows the general way of doing business and the way value is delivered by the industry.

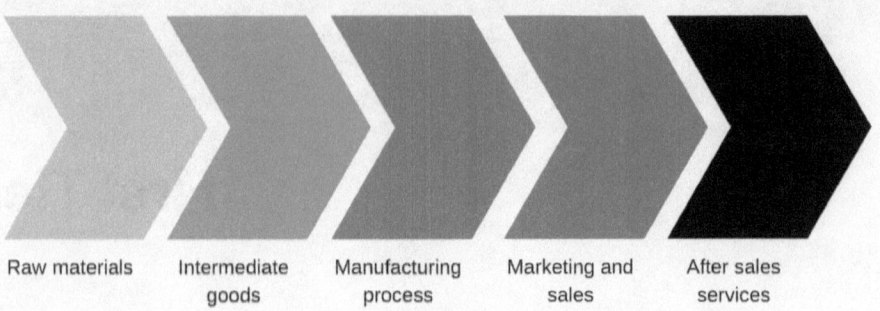

This is a general flow of activities for each industry. Steps and activities relating to each level in the production process must be listed down.

INDUSTRY'S VALUE CHAIN

| Raw materials | Intermediate goods | Manufacturing process | Marketing and sales | After sales services |

The industry's value chain is a generic set of activities done at each stage—right from procurement of raw materials to the activities done after sale (after-sales service once the sale is made). The industry value chain does not look at firm-specific activities but only looks at the generic activities required to create and deliver the promised product or service. Analysts must identify the activities that are most critical for successful delivery of value. For instance, research and development abilities of pharmaceutical companies, risk management and distribution capabilities of insurance companies, procurement costs for manufacturing companies. The industry's value chain helps identify all activities to be performed and those of critical importance for success within the industry.

At the company level, the value chain analysis helps better understand the activities that lead to competitive advantage. One can begin with the generic value chain and then identify the relevant firm-specific activities.[2]

---

[2]   http://aronkiptarus.blogspot.com/2012/10/the-value-chain.html

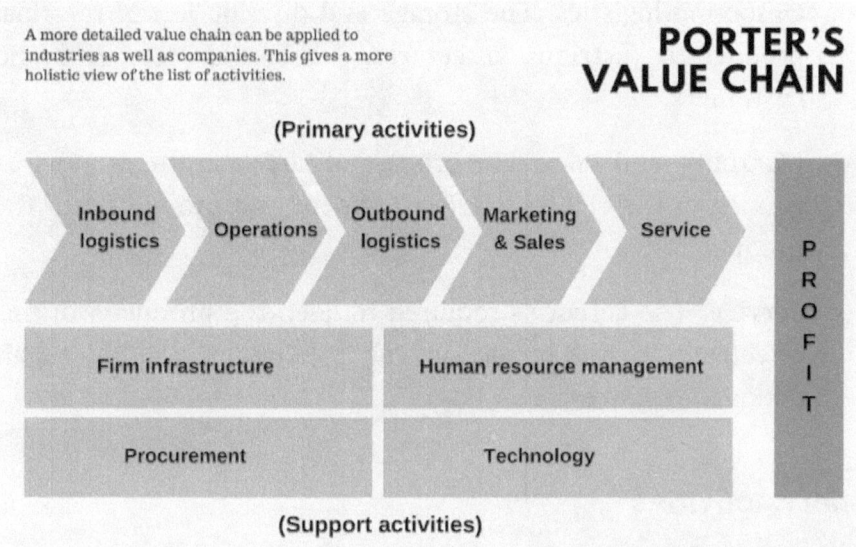

A more detailed value chain can be applied to industries as well as companies. This gives a more holistic view of the list of activities.

The firm-specific value chain model is the one proposed by Michael Porter in 1985. He categorised all activities performed by a firm as primary activities or support activities. Primary activities add value directly to the production, i.e. they contribute directly in transforming inputs into outputs. Support activities are those that are required at the firm level; they support execution of primary activities rather than directly contribute to the production process.

Primary Activities

- Inbound logistics: The process of receiving raw materials or parts from the suppliers and storing them for the production process

- Operations: The process of converting inputs into the final product or service

- Outbound logistics: The storage and distribution of the final product to distribution centres, wholesalers, retailers and customers

- Marketing and sales: The process of targeting the product or service to the right customer segment and promotion of the product

- Service: The activities required to keep the product working effectively for the buyer, such as installation, training, repair and maintenance[3]

Support Activities

- Technology development: Research to determine how the company can use technology to automate processes and develop new products

- Human resource management: The activities involved with recruiting, training and retaining the employees needed

- Procurement: The sourcing of raw materials at the correct cost and quality

- Firm infrastructure: The activities involved with the company's structure, management, planning, accounting and finances[3]

All the primary and secondary activities mapped together, for each company, allow the analyst to identify and compare the activities performed and thus understand the differences that lead to differentiation and cost advantages. The industry value chain can also be replaced by a sum of primary activities performed by the various companies.

---

[3]   https://www.lucidchart.com/blog/what-is-value-chain-analysis

The value chain does not directly help understand the quality of the industry but it helps understand how the industry operates. This will be useful in the analysis of the industry and the companies operating in it. Value chain analysis is a popular model for analysis at the company level.

Firstly, whichever industry is selected, an industry value chain must be created. This can be done using the industry value chain model or the primary activities of the Porter's value chain model. Then one must identify the activities that are critical to success in the industry. Once this is done, a value chain must be designed for individual companies in the industry. Then analysts must compare and contrast the individual value chains with each other and with that of the industry. Company value chains that are very identical to the industry value chain (or similar to the value chains of most companies) will seldom have exceptional returns. They will make average returns in the industry. It is the value chains that are significantly different from that of the industry and other companies that have room for relative cost or differentiation advantage. These companies are competitively advantaged or disadvantaged and clock above-average or below-average returns.

Firm infrastructure - R&D centers, SAP and ERP for organisation, database of farmers, tie-ups with universities

Human resource management - Employee management teams, college referral schemes, internal promotions, on-field staff training

Tech development - Tie-ups with other companies and colleges, in-house R&D division, global innovators tie-up, product and application development e.g. molecule design, route synthesis

Procurement - Dedicated team for procurement near manufacturing setups

Inbound logistics -	Operations -	Outbound logistics	Marketing and	Service - Customer
Tie-ups with logistics companies	Registrations of new products, manufacturing of finished products, licensing agreements with others	- Tie-ups with logistics players and 3PL players; multiple stock points at depots and C&F agents; hub and spoke distribution used	sales - Brand recognition programmes, global presence initiatives, exclusive distribution rights, etc	connect initiatives, community engagement programmes, field force, helpline numbers, etc.

VALUE CHAIN OF AGROCHEMICAL INDUSTRY

What it means

All the players in the industry need to perform a combination of these activities to operate in the industry. These are the activities that need to be taken care of. It is the ability of different companies to perform these activities better than others that determines their strength.

Analysts and practitioners must understand the activities that the industry needs and which are the more critical ones. Only then can they evaluate the strengths and weaknesses of the companies.

How to benefit from it

Each activity is a source of differentiation for the companies in the industry. The companies can choose to do any combination of activities they wish to and get the rest outsourced with differing implications on the competitive positioning of the company.

The companies can also choose to do activities that are outside the value chain, which might give them a source of differentiation and benefit from the position.

Those wanting to start a business in the industry must understand value chain as a chain of activities that they will need to perform and how capable they are of performing these activities.

Value System

No industry operates in a vacuum. Industries are linked to each other as suppliers or customers. The industry's value chain is linked to the value chain of upstream supplier industries and downstream buyer industries. The result is a larger stream of activities known as the value system. In a value system, changes in any of the industry's value chain affect the other value chains, and the ultimate delivery of values at each level is altered.[4]

Similarly, at the firm level as well, companies, along with their suppliers and buyers, are part of a larger value system. When there are changes in the activities performed by any of the participants of the value system, there is a need for adjustments by all other players of the value system.

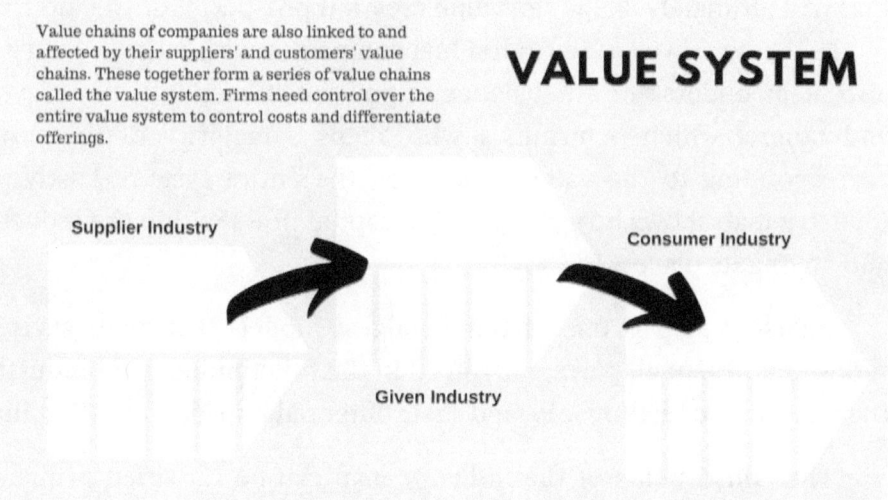

Value chains of companies are also linked to and affected by their suppliers' and customers' value chains. These together form a series of value chains called the value system. Firms need control over the entire value system to control costs and differentiate offerings.

VALUE SYSTEM

Supplier Industry

Consumer Industry

Given Industry

Analysts should try to not just understand the given value chain but also aim for an understanding of the entire value system. This holistic view allows them to identify changes anywhere in the value chain and

[4]   https://mpra.ub.uni-muenchen.de/66799/8/MPRA_paper_66799.pdf

value system and the implications that the changes can have on the industry or the companies of their interest.

#2 Industry Map

Michael J. Mauboussin and Dan Callahan identified the concept of industry map in their ground-breaking paper 'Measuring the Moat'. They identify it as a visual representation of all players in an industry— suppliers, manufacturers, distributors, consultants, influencers, regulators, dealers and customers, and how money, products and services change hands within the industry.

The goal of an industry map is to identify the kind of economic relationship that the industry has with all support industries and institutions. It helps understand the current and potential interactions that will ultimately shape the value creation prospects for the industry on the whole as well as for individual companies within the industry. It also helps understand the balance of power between industry players and others, which determines who keeps a majority of the profit corresponding to the value created by the entire system. Lastly, an industry map shows how the working capital flows within the industry and among its players.[5]

Industry map is one of the strongest models that gives a visual representation of all players involved in the functioning of an industry, their economic relationship, and their potential impact on profitability.

The constituents of the industry map can be classified primarily into three—suppliers, customers and external forces. The map should identify all the constituents and companies that may influence profitability. It should also identify the various companies that are dominant in the related industries.

---

[5]   http://analystreports.som.yale.edu/internal/F2013/MJ/Measuring%20the%20 Moat.pdf

An illustration of an industry map is shown below.

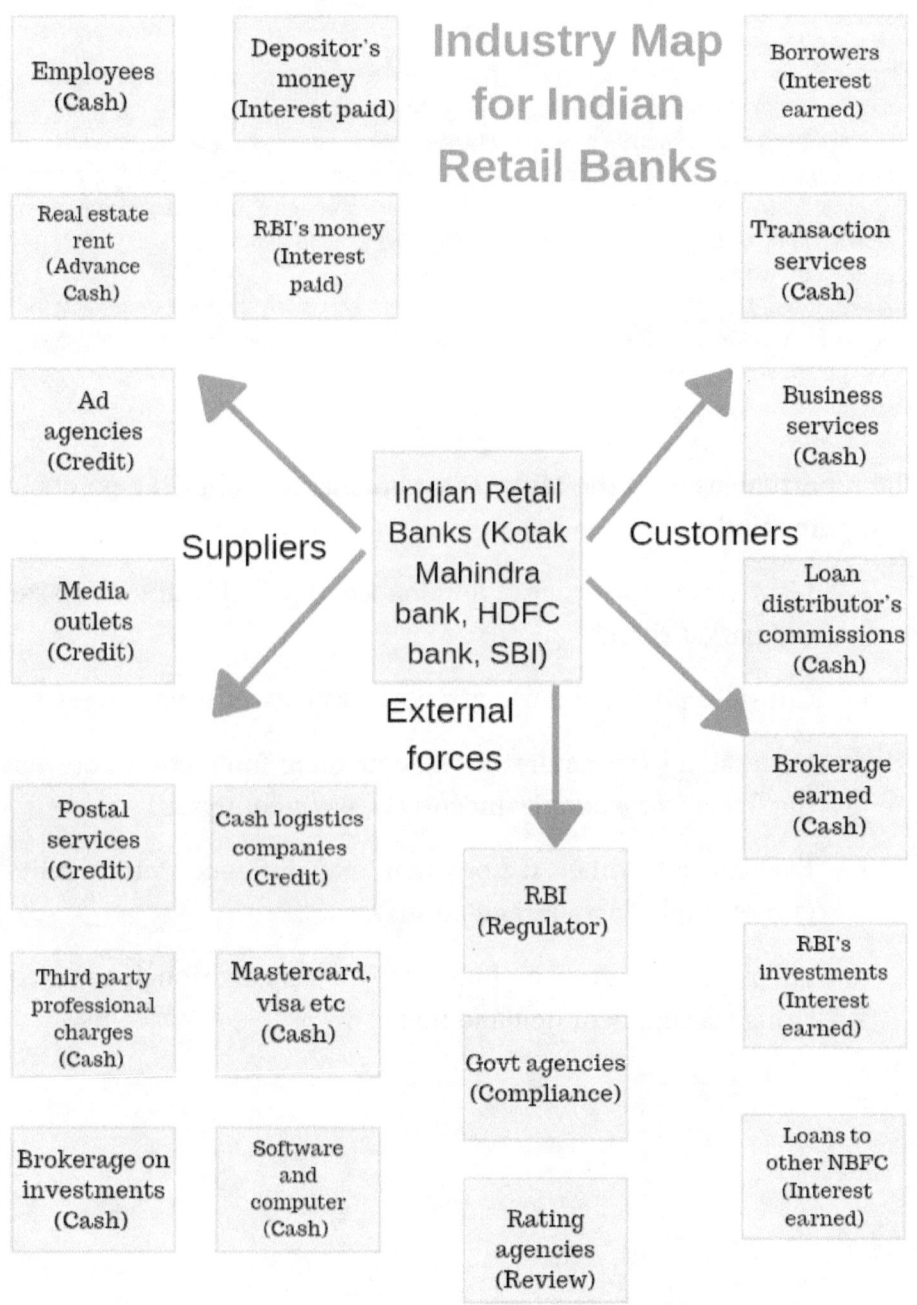

Explaining the industry map

The diagram shows the industry map for retail banks in India. It includes the various suppliers and buyers with whom the companies in the industry need to interact. It shows the kind of economic relation the industry shares with others. It can be used to evaluate the various forces and the impact that they have on the industry.

The same can also be used to understand the cash flow cycle of the industry. It shows whether expenses are cash or credit and similarly incomes are cash or credit. It also is an indiactor company's bargaining power over suppliers and competitors.

Practitioners and analysts need to understand the map, as changes in any of these industries can affect the industry. It helps track and better understand the changes.

The report 'Measuring the Moat' recommends the following points to be kept in mind:

- List firms in the order of dominance, typically defined as 'size' or 'market share'.

- Consider potential new entrants as well as existing players.

- Understand the nature of the economic interaction between the firms (for example: incentives, payment terms).

- Evaluate any other factors that may influence profitability (for example: labour, regulations).

- Shocks to one firm or industry can ripple through to other firms via supply or demand links.

Industry Map for Indian Express Logistics Industry

Employees (Cash)

Truck owners (Cash)

Software and computer (Cash)

Truck maintenance (Cash)

B2B customers (Credit 45- 90 days)

Building and maintenance (Cash)

Agents / Brokers (Credit 30-60 days)

Suppliers

Express logistics companies in India (TCI express, Gati express, safexpress etc)

Customers

Third party freight operators (Credit - 30 days)

Tie up with other logistics co. (Credit 20-30 days)

External forces

Air freight operators (Credit - 30 days)

Fuel (Cash)

B2C and ecommerce services (Credit 20-30 days)

Government (Regulations)

Labour boards (Cash)

Brokers for trucks (Cash)

Branch bookings (Cash)

Warehouse owners - Rent (Cash)

Warehouse equipments (Cash)

Industry Map for Indian Premier League teams

Players
(Cash)

Broadcasters
(Advance cash)

Support staff
(Cash)

Ticket sales
distributor
(Cash)

Logistics
(Cash)

Ticket sales
(Cash)

Suppliers

Indian Premier
League Teams
(Chennai Super
Kings, Kolkata
Knight Riders etc)

Customers

Accomodation
(Credit)

Food and
beverages
sales
(Cash)

**External
Forces**

Marketing
agencies
(Credit)

Sponsors
(Advance
Cash)

Tournament
organiser -
Franchise fee
(Cash)

IPL governing
body
(Regulator)

Merchandising
sales
(Credit)

Stadium
(Advance
Cash)

BCCI
(Compliance)

Team's TV
shows and
events rights
(Advance)

#3 Profit Pool

Once the activities, support companies and constituents of the industry are understood, it is important to identify where and how money is being made in the industry. Some questions need to be answered. *Which value chain activities are the most profitable? Where are the differences in the patterns of revenue and profit concentration? How do some players in the industry exert influence over the remaining players and shape competition?* The answers to these questions are found in an important analytical tool called 'profit pool'. It is a method conceived by Orit Gadiesh and James L. Gilbert, consultants at Bain & Co.

Profit pool is an analytical tool that compares profitability and size in terms of revenue, for each of the value chain activities in the industry. It is a visual representation, wherein the x axis constitutes the size of the activity, in terms of revenue, and the y axis constitutes the operational margin. Profit pool focusses on forces and distribution of profits in the industry. It is a departure from the managerial strategy that focusses on revenues instead of profit, assuming that revenue growth will eventually translate into profit growth. It helps identify the activities that are generating disproportionately large or small shares of profits.[6]

Before conducting a profit pool analysis, one must define the pool. This refers to defining the boundaries by identifying the value chain activities that are relevant to the analysis and within the scope of the industry. For the purpose of analysis and developing a strategy, where should the value chain begin and end? For example, for e-commerce marketplaces, including manufacturing activities in the pool may not be directly relevant. However, for a manufacturer who sells through these e-commerce marketplaces, it is relevant to add manufacturing as well as selling activities in the pool.

Once the profit pool activities have been identified, the size of each activity, in terms of revenue and the matching profitability, needs to

---

[6]   https://www.science.gov/topicpages/t/triga+mark-iii+pool.html

be identified. The challenge here is that the reporting requirements of the companies do not require them to report activity-wise data. Also, companies carry out a combination of activities, thus making the process of obtaining activity-wise numbers a complex one. The process is then a matter of aggregating and disaggregating.

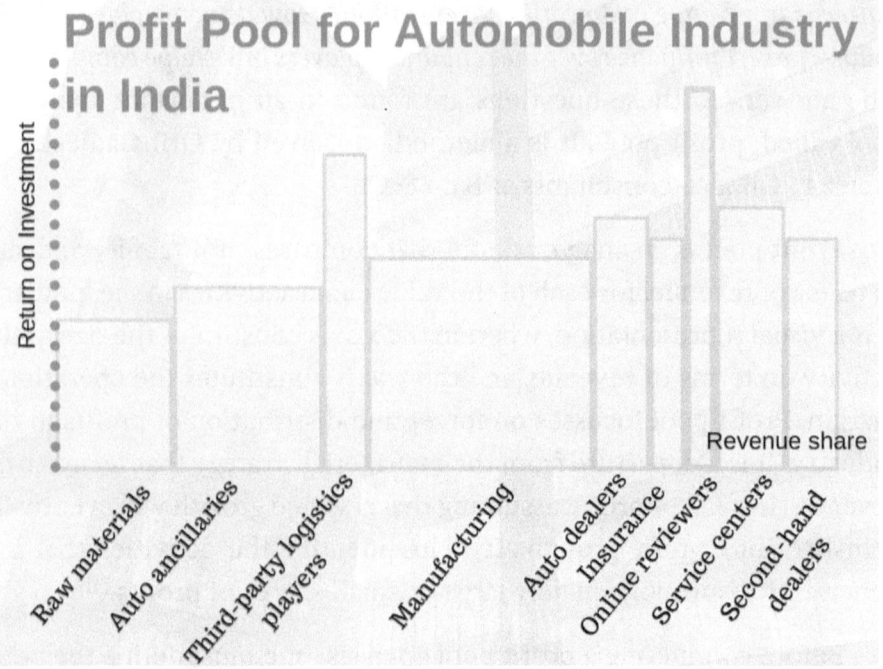

Profit Pool for Automobile Industry in India

How to create profit pool and how to benefit from it

Firstly, the scope of value chain is decided. It includes the activities that are to be included in the profit pool.

Next, size and profitability of each activity is identified. If exact value cannot be obtained, an estimate is used.

It is then plotted on the graph to see which activity is the most attractive to do and which shall be left out.

For more details, each activity can be broken down further.

Analysts and practitioners should use a profit pool to identify how big companies can become performing certain activities and what returns they can expect to earn. It is a very powerful tool while the business model of the company is being developed.

Here, 3PL and online reviewers are the most attractive businesses return-wise. However, manufacturing and auto ancillaries are the biggest in terms of size. Thus, it becomes a trade-off between size and returns.

The first step in the analysis is identifying the 'pure' players carrying out only a particular activity. The activity profitability can be estimated by aggregating the profits of pure players. Then the mixed players are identified, i.e. those who perform many different activities. Each company's financial data and disclosures are disaggregated to arrive at estimates for each specific activity. By combining data from pure players as well as mixed players, an estimate of the size and profitability of activities is established. The profit pool is then analysed. Why have the profit pools formed where they have? Are the forces that created these pools likely to change? Will new and more profitable business models emerge? These questions are looked into.

The shape of the profit pool is usually complex and reflects the competitive dynamics of the industry. Even very competitive industries with generally low profitability can have certain activities with high profitability. However, the profitability of any particular activity in the pool may vary with customer group, product category, geographical market and distribution channel. Thus, carrying out a profit pool analysis allows the analyst to understand how profit is distributed and which are the profit areas.

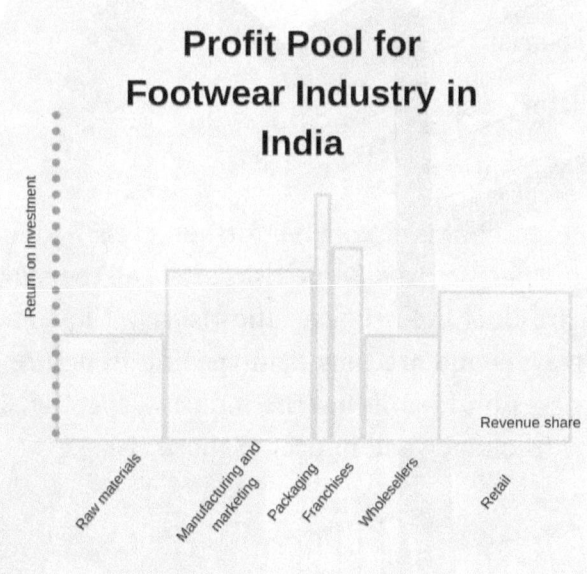

#4 Major Industry Risks

Risk refers to any form of uncertainty that affects the business positively or negatively. Almost all businesses have some form of uncertainty or the other and are thus affected by the risks. Risks vary in the frequency with which they occur and the impact they may have once they occur. They affect a business's ability to operate directly or indirectly. Risks can come from within the business or firm; they can be internal or external, i.e. come from outside the business (from the business environment).

Some internal risk factors that affect the business:

- Operational risk

- Legal risk

- Supply chain risks

- Human factor risk

Some external risk factors that affect the business:

- Interest rate risk

- Political risk

- Regulatory risk

- Environment risk

Internal and external risks can be further classified into industry-specific or firm-specific risks. Some risks affect all the players in a given industry and are thus industry-specific risks, while some risks affect only certain players and are thus firm-specific in nature. This section primarily focusses on identifying the industry-specific risks and tries to evaluate the frequency and impact of these risks.

One of the simple, yet powerful risk management models is the Robson risk management model. Created by Dr Linda M. Robson, the model was first created to identify and control industry-specific risks affecting the events industry.

The first step—personal risk perception—is for practitioners in any industry. It focusses on identification of any activity within the industry that is perceived to increase the uncertainty of outcome. Different activities can be perceived with varying levels of risks by different people. Analysts have the task of identifying activities that are perceived to be potentially risky. This task involves creating a list of activities and factors that may or may not be risky in reality but is perceived to be risky. The source of information can be primary as well as secondary. Practitioners (entrepreneurs, business managers) and analysts may collect data from industry publications, commentaries by various management experts, journals, or government statistics. They can also rely on first-hand experience within the industry.[7]

The risk identification phase requires the use of resources to create a more holistic and inclusive list of potential risks associated with the industry. It involves evaluation of risks that were initially perceived to be risky, whether they are risky or not in reality. This phase is carried out in conjunction with the personal risk perception phase. It eliminates activities or factors that are perceived to be risky but in reality are not risky. This phase gives a list of risks that actually affect the industry as output.[7]

After this comes the risk assessment phase, which focusses on assessing the levels of risks for the various risks identified in the previous phase. The level of risk is based on the severity and frequency of impact.

[7] https://www.specialevents.com/blog/creative-approach-risk-management-robson-risk-management-model

Level of Risk = Consequence of Risk x Likelihood

LIKELIHOOD SCALE FOR RISK

Level	Likelihood	Description
4	Very likely	Happens more than once a year in the industry
3	Likely	Happens about once a year in the industry
2	Unlikely	Happens every 10 years or more in the industry
1	Very unlikely	Has only happened once in the industry

Consequences of Risk

Consequence of risk	Severity of consequences
4	Severe
3	High
2	Moderate
1	Low

The consequence of the risk is evaluated subjectively. It can be made more objective by defining each stage. The basis of the division can be financial loss, customer loss or team morale loss. A quantitative representation of the impact of risk is obtained by multiplying the scale of likelihood and the consequence of risk. The following table can be used to assess the level of risk.

Level of Risk

Level of risk	Description
12 - 16	Severe
8 - 12	High
4 - 8	Moderate
1 - 4	Low

Level of risk = Likelihood level x Consequence level

Once the risk has been assessed, its frequency and severity of impact have been understood, the next phase focusses on risk strategies—that is developing policies and procedures for dealing with risks, both before and after they happen.

Strategy for Risk

Level of risk	Strategy
Severe	Avoid
High	Transfer
Moderate	Reduce
Low	Accept

- Avoid risks that occur very frequently and have significant consequences. Firms must find a way to avoid risks that affect their survival. Accepting such risks would lead to constant hiccups on the path of growth.

- Transfer risks that have significant consequences but do not occur very frequently. Transfer them to others (insurance company, outsourced partner, JV partner etc) by paying a premium for the transfer. Some ways to transfer a risk to another party are through insurance, outsourcing, joint ventures or partnerships.

- Reduce risks that have moderate consequences. The likelihood and the consequences of risk should be reduced through active measures. This can be done in the following ways.

- First, by reducing the likelihood of the risk happening; for example, through quality control, staff training or auditing.

- Second, by reducing the impact if the risk occurs; for example, through emergency procedures and minimising exposures to sources of risk. Accept risks that do not occur frequently and leave a minimal impact. Such risks are best accepted the way they are; no active effort is utilised in reducing such risks.

Various risk levels have different ideal strategies. However, not all strategies are feasible in each situation. For instance, a risk that must be transferred may find itself being accepted due to a firm's inability to transfer it. Each of the risks should be understood and appropriate strategies should be designed. For example, geographical concentration risk is a huge risk for firms in insurance industry. However, the large firms are able to diversify away such risks whereas the smaller ones are not able to reduce such risks.

A firm's ability or disability to carry out the ideal strategy for each of the industry risks affects its competitive position. However, a firm may actively choose to deviate from the ideal strategy for competitive reasons. Firms might make a decision to insure risks that others accept or completely reject risks that others insure. Also, some firms may find themselves in a position to reduce or avoid risks that others cannot and thus be placed at a position of advantage compared to others.

The last phase of the risk management process is 'risk evaluation'. This phase focusses on whether the risk management process is effective or not. It ensures that each step is carried out properly—the major risks are identified and assessed and then the correct strategies are implemented. The challenges to the entire process are identified along with feedback. This phase is more applicable for practitioners rather than analysts.

The primary purpose of the industry risk analysis in the first tier of the broad industry analysis is not to identify firms that are placed at an advantage or a disadvantage or how they individually tackle the risks. The primary purpose is to identify the major risks affecting an industry, assess their level, and finally figure out what can be done about them. If a particular industry faces severe or high-level risks and most of the players in the industry cannot avoid them or transfer them and are forced to accept them, then it may be best to avoid the industry as a whole. For example, smaller banks that lend only to a particular industry or a particular geography are best avoided as these have huge loan book concentration risks. The riskiness of operations in the industry can be judged based on identifying these individual risks and ascertaining the ideal versus actual response to them.

One form of risk that affects almost all industries in varying degrees is the risk of disruptions. This particular risk threatens the very existence of an industry in the form of newer business models and stronger value propositions. Firms in all industries have to be constantly on the lookout for such risks. This particular risk must be evaluated in greater depth in the second tier of the broad industry analysis. All other industry risks are understood and evaluated at this stage.

Risks Identified	Likelihood	Severity	Risk Rating
Seasonal fluctuations, climatic variations and rainfall	3	3	9
Customers unable to pay debt due to local economic conditions	3	3	9
Risk of not getting all the required approvals	3	2	6
Brand image among farmers being hurt	2	3	6
Slow industry growth	3	3	9
Fluctuations in price of commodities	2	3	6
Counterfeit products	4	3	12
Inadequate R&D pipeline	3	2	6
Social resistance against use of agrochem	2	4	8

Risks for Indian Agrochemical Companies

Major risks for agrochemical industry include local seasonal and climatic factors, local economic conditions, counterfeit products and slow industry growth, leading to cut-throat competition.

Local factors affect all agrochem companies that are regional in nature. However, UPL Ltd, the largest Indian agrochemical company, can avoid almost all local risks such as seasonal fluctuations and geography-based risks. This is because the company operates in 6 continents and the effects and fluctuations of local factors across the regions get neutralised. As a result, UPL is better equipped to handle risks than its local peers.

Risks Identified	Likelihood	Severity	Risk Rating
Any mishap can affect bank's reputation considerably	3	3	9
Concentration in loan book of any kind - customer-wise, geography-wise, industry-wise	2	3	6
Increase in NPA due to faulty credit appraisal process	3	2	6
Affected by macro-economics and market forces	2	3	6
Asset-liability mismatch	3	3	9
Interest rate risks	4	3	12
Frauds with the system or cyber attacks	3	3	9
Digital platforms may affect intermediate's commissions	3	2	6
Regulatory compliance changes	2	4	8

Risks for Indian Retail Banks

The above risks have been identified after listing down all the risks that were initially perceived to be risky. They were individually analysed and those that were not found risky were eliminated. This refers to identification stage for risks. The major source of information includes draft red herring prospectus and discussions with various analysts.

Based on research, many risks are not too frequent or not too severe. The most important risks that the industry faces include loan book concentration risks, credit appraisal process and asset-liability mismatch.

These risks are most critical ones for the performance of all players in the industry. These cannot be ignored by any player.

Individual firms have different capabilities to strategise for the risk which determine their competitive position.

For example,
1. Kotak Mahindra Bank and HDFC Bank have negligible concentration risks. It is well spread out over products, geographies and industries.
2. ILF&S was running an asset-liability mismatch. This was mainly because of long-term infra projects being financed by short-term loans.

Differing business models and value propositions affect each player's ability to treat risk. It affects the competitive position of the firms.

#5 Demand-Supply Scenario in Industry

All industries have their profitability determined by the demand and supply forces affecting the industry, whether they are seasonal, cyclical or structural. The impact of undercapacity as well as overcapacity is felt across different firms in the industry. How industries move from undercapacity to overcapacity and back to undercapacity can be very well understood from the commodity cycle. The movement and behaviour of firms is pretty much the same as it is in the commodity cycle, though with varying time horizons.

The five phases of the commodity cycle are:

1. In phase 1, an increase in demand of the commodity-related input causes it to exceed its supply. When demand exceeds supply, price and profitability rise. The surge in demand relates to economic growth, increased innovation or basic economics where lower prices lead to higher demand.[8]

2. As prices start rising, more producers see their margins expand. This calls for larger capital spending to increase production as well as fresh entry from outsiders. During this time, prices continue to rise higher, thus continuously inviting fresh capital. Such price and output movement can be clearly seen in most commodities such as crude oil, aluminium and cement.[8]

3. As capital expenditure ramps up, capacity is increased. This brings more supply into the market. At the same time, higher prices begin to erode market demand. High prices also encourage substitution.[8]

4. The next phase begins once supply from new production overwhelms demand and prices begin to fall. This hurts profitability.[8]

5. Once the reality of lower prices hits the market, capital expenditure is tapered or discontinued completely to avoid

producing unprofitably. This fall in profitability causes many players to exit the field. This drain of supply from the market creates a new equilibrium that becomes a cyclical bottom. Once the capacity reduces, it provides space for undercapacity and picks up profitability, and the cycle turns around, as stage one repeats itself.[8]

This is the manner in which profitability of most industries move, based on demand and supply. The tenure of the cycle and the variability of the industry may vary, but the pattern of the cycle remains the same. The cycle is spread out over years and there is no definite point where the industry can be said to move from one phase to another. Also, while understanding the demand-supply dynamics of the industry, along with the cyclical factors, the structural and seasonal factors affecting demand and supply should also be understood. To understand the demand-supply scenario, analysts as well as practitioners must carry out the following steps.

- Demand forecasting

- Supply capacity analysis

- Capacity utilisation

- Supply strategies

Demand Forecasting

One of the pivotal factors that influence the profitability of any industry is the demand for the industry's product. Demand forecasting happens when historical sales data is used to develop an estimate of the future customer demand. It is an estimate of the amount of goods and services the industry's customers will purchase. It is one of the important

---

[8]   https://www.daytrading.com/commodity-cycle

functions as strategic and operational plans are devised around the forecasted demand.

Demand forecasting can be broadly classified into the level of detailing, timespan considered, and the scope of market being forecasted.

Level of detailing: Passive forecasting is carried out for stable businesses with very conservative growth plans. Active forecasting is carried out for businesses with aggressive growth plans and it includes a much greater level of detailing; for instance, product analysis or competitor analysis.[9]

Timespan: Demand forecasting and analysis can be done for the short, medium and long terms.

Short-term demand forecasting is carried out for a period of 3–12 months, and it helps evaluate year-specific and seasonal demand for the product. Seasonality must be carefully evaluated, as it is a recurring phenomenon.

Medium-term forecasting is carried out for a period of more than 12 months till 36 months. This helps evaluate the demand against the capacity in the industry and where the industry is placed cyclically. This helps evaluate cyclicality of the industry profitability.

Long-term forecasting is carried out for a period of more than 36 months. This is more structural in nature, as, in the long run, the effects of seasonality and cyclicality are neutralised. Long-term forecasting focusses more on survival of the industry, its evolution and the effects of disruption.[9]

[9]   https://blog.arkieva.com/demand-forecasting/

Scope of Market

Macro level demand forecasting focusses more on the demand from consumers at the macro level, which means at the level of the economy or the industry. Business level demand forecasting focusses on firm-specific demand, based on factors such as product category, sales division and financial division.

Indicators of Demand

Demand analysis and forecasting is not an exact science but is a subjective practice, with various methods being used with differing levels of success. Irrespective of the method used, the ultimate objective for both B2B and B2C business is to understand the end-customer demand based on the demographics of the customer segment and the buying environment. Forecasting demand is an exercise to collect cues and trends from multiple sources. Then they are compiled together to form an analysis or forecast the demand from the end consumer. These hints are indicators of demand and they help the analyst or the practitioner stay ahead of the demand.

One of the most important indicators of demand is the demand forecast and demand scenario for the backward (suppliers) and forward (customers) industries in the value chain. The inventory levels of such industries help identify the demand scenario. As all these industries cater to the same end-customer demand, the industry demand for each of them is highly correlated. The demand forecast of these industries can be identified by the communication from the management of these companies. Also, the demand of these companies can be tracked by their staff recruitment in recent times, outgoing and incoming logistics, and capacity additions. However, getting all the requisite information about the industries and companies is a challenge, and analysts need to resort to creative practices to get the required information.

Inventory levels and changes in inventory level across the value chain is an important indicator of demand. Backward and forward firms with rising raw material levels indicate that firms are positive about the industry demand in the short run. However, firms with a rising finished product inventory show slowing demand. Inventory levels are also indicative of business optimism across channels.

One of the methods to keep track of the end customer is to conduct a detailed market research and develop key variables that drive the industry demand in that particular industry. For instance, automobile sales is directly affected by liquidity and lending rates in financial markets. In India, monsoon affects the end-consumer demand for automobiles. New vehicle launches also affect the demand for automobiles. Once these factors have been identified, companies should keep track of these variables and conduct regular end-customer analysis. This would help the players stay ahead of the demand in the industry and regularly update the customer profile.

While analysing industry demand, it is very important to constantly evaluate the impact of substitutes and industrial disruption forces affecting the industry. If the substitutes seem to be offering better value at a lower price, the industry demand may take a hit. The firms in the industry should keep track of the value proposition and demand for these substitutes. This helps them decide how to adapt and whether to participate in the substitute industry. This will influence the demand scenario in a favourable manner for the firm.

Also, new products, new business models, and new value chains affect the industry and generally in an irreversible manner. These changes can take away the demand from traditional businesses and concentrate it towards the newer ones within the same industry. Thus, it is imperative for an analyst to stay ahead of such disruptive forces to have an understanding of the demand. The bottom line while analysing substitutes and disruptions is that the business/firm with a stronger value proposition for the customers will attract demand.

Other factors that indicate demand include the pricing within the industry and its impact on demand, based on price elasticity. An industry's growth can be in terms of value or volume or both. Industries with high price elasticity find it difficult to increase prices and generally grow only in volume terms. However, industries with low elasticity of price can keep increasing prices and yet find volume growth. For example, most consumer electronics grow in volume terms only without much increase in price due to their price elasticity. They are able to increase prices only when a new innovative product is launched. However, inelastic items such as medicines are able to grow in volume as well as value terms over time. The price of the product is evaluated along with the value proposition, so that the industry offers a stronger value proposition over its substitutes. Another factor that affects long-term demand of a product is the change in industry dynamics. For instance, more players entering a new industry causes more advertisement and thus increases long-term demand for the product.

While forecasting demand, analysts use primary as well as secondary sources of data. They may conduct on-ground research and administer questionnaires or use secondary sources like interviews, journals and articles. Survey is an effective primary as well as secondary source of data. For analysts and practitioners, however, it is very easy to be biased and fall prey to wishful thinking, which takes them away from the reality of the demand scenario. Thus, all forecasting should have an objective and quantitative basis to some extent, combined with general surveys that are subjective in nature.

DEMAND ANALYSIS FOR INDIAN CEMENT INDUSTRY

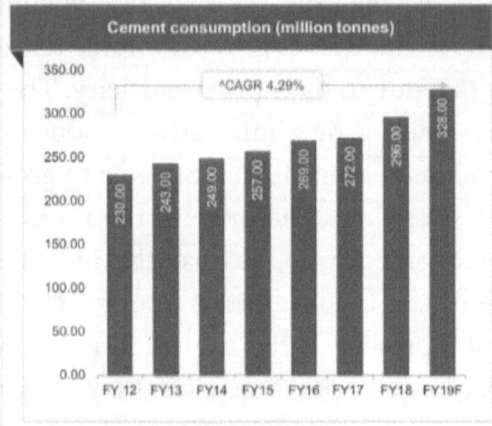

Cement consumption (million tonnes)

^CAGR 4.29%

Values: FY12 230.00, FY13 243.00, FY14 249.00, FY15 257.00, FY16 269.00, FY17 272.00, FY18 296.00, FY19F 328.00

- Cement consumption has grown at a CAGR of 4.3% since 2012.
- The industry is expected to grow 6-8% in volume terms till FY25.
- Growth drivers going forward:
1. Government initiatives going forward (Smart cities, PMAY) and push on infrastructure
2. Strong growth in rural housing
3. Favourable demographics
4. Rising demand in industrial sector

Source: IBEF report on cement industry - July 2019

- The method used for such basic demand analysis is secondary research from industry research reports. However, this has also been confirmed from individual management commentary.
- There is no substitute for cement. Prices are determined in commodity markets, which are region specific.
- **So, we can conclude that the cement industry has a stable and steady demand growth outlook.**

Supply Capacity Analysis

Once an understanding of the industry demand is established, the learnings must be brought together with an understanding of the industry supply to determine profitability. The first step in analysing the industry's supply is to analyse the industry's current supply. Analysts must collect information about the current supply capacity in the industry in volume terms and the technological status of this capacity. Once an understanding of the current supply has been established, analysts must research the capacity that will arise in the near future. This concerns the ongoing and planned capital expenditure by the players in the industry. The challenge with such an analysis is the availability of the required information. For industries with a few large firms, data can be collected by adding the supply and capital expenditure plans of the firms. However, for industries that are fragmented in nature, the availability of information still remains a challenge. Therefore, analysts must rely on information available in journals, newspapers, magazines, industry reports, and government statistics. If supply capacity cannot be ascertained, analysts can get a sense of the demand-supply scenario using the capacity utilisation levels across the smaller firms in the fragmented industry. Capital expenditure plans can be judged by the sales and order book of capital goods companies that provide the assets for expansion of the industry.

Another important factor to analyse is the lead time for new capacity to come up. The industry's profitability moves in a cycle, similar to the commodity cycle, as shown earlier, and the time taken for the industry to switch between phases depends on the time taken for capacity to enter and exit the industry. If the lead time is high, the industry will enjoy a phase of high profitability—where the demand is greater than the supply for a longer period of time. Then it moves to the next phase where the supply catches up, thus reducing profitability. For industries where the time between capital expenditure planning and production start is less, the change in profitability due to demand-supply scenario is quick.

Another factor that needs to be analysed is the requirement of new capacity and availability of resources. Adding capacity requires all factors of production—land at the correct location, labour with relevant skills, adequate financing at adequate rates, and relevant physical capital. Availability of all the resources in the required quantity often becomes a challenge and sometimes even a hindrance to capacity expansion. Also, some resources are available only to a few select players in the industry. For instance, there may be a shortage of employees with certain requisite skills to operate a particular kind of machine. These are, what we call, expansion constraints. For analysts, it is important to identify the expansion constraints and their impact on the industry's supply and profitability.

A factor very closely linked to expansion constraints is barriers to entry. Barriers to entry in an industry are those factors that do not allow the entry of new players to the industry; they may even make expansion difficult for existing players. For instance, network effects in a social media company or economies of scale leading to cost advantages for a manufacturing company are barriers to entry. These factors make it difficult for supply to increase quickly and cause the existing players to enjoy greater profitability for a longer period of time. Some of the factors that lead to high barriers of entry in an industry are brand loyalty, geography barriers, intellectual property rights, and economies of scale. Analysts must identify the barriers to entry in an industry, as they make it difficult to add new capacity quickly, thus allowing existing players to earn superior profitability for long.

Analysts should also keep track of the supply scenario of substitute product industries. Substitute industries that are building new supply capacity may offer the product at a lower price, going ahead, and there may be a point where the value proposition of the substitutes becomes stronger than that of the given industry. This would lead to a shift in demand from the given industry to the substitute industry and thus make the demand-supply scenario unfavourable to the industry by building overcapacity. Analysts and practitioners should keep a close track of the substitute product industry's supply scenario. However, the ability of the customers to switch to the substitute industry is determined by an important factor called switching costs. Switching costs refer to the costs for the buyer while switching to a substitute product, against the benefits received with switching.

Some causes of high switching costs:

- Financial cost

- Hassle (psychological pain)

- Habit

- Complexity in usage

- Technology and technical know-how

- Knowledge and training

- Compatibility of two products

- Prior data with the company

Analysts must identify the switching costs, as high switching costs limit the ability of a substitute product to take away demand from any given industry.

The final factors that should be analysed are exit of firms from an industry and the exit barriers along with it. As supply begins to overwhelm demand and prices begin to fall, firms lose their profitability. Some industries even become loss-making ones, thus encouraging exits by multiple players. This exit by players limits supply with an industry and thus restores profitability for the remaining firms. However, the ability of firms to exit the business and reduce supply is determined by the exit barriers in the industry and the time taken to exit.

Some common exit barriers:

- Investment in specialist equipment that cannot really be used in other industries tends to be an impediment to leaving the industry.

- Highly specialised skills by industry participants that cannot be utilised in other industries impede exits from the industry.

- High levels of dedicated fixed costs may also be an impediment to leaving the industry.

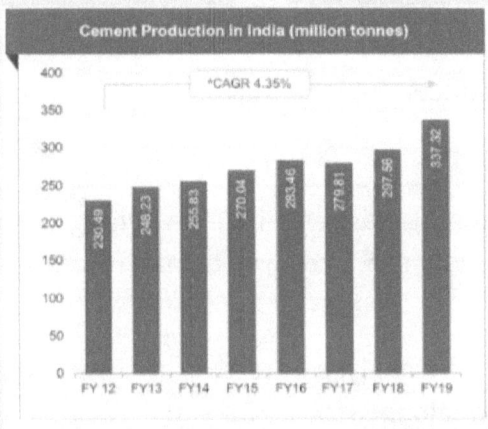

SUPPLY ANALYSIS FOR INDIAN CEMENT INDUSTRY

Cement Production in India (million tonnes)

*CAGR 4.35%

FY12: 230.49, FY13: 248.23, FY14: 255.83, FY15: 270.04, FY16: 283.46, FY17: 279.81, FY18: 297.56, FY19: 337.32

- Cement production has grown at a CAGR of 4.35% since FY12.
- The industry supply is expected to increase in line with demand.
- It takes a few months for new supply to come up. It cannot come up very quickly.
- New supply depends on limestone reserve availability. However, there is ample idle capacity to incentivise less aggressive expansion plans by companies.
- Also, cement plants are very capital expensive. So a new outside entry is difficult.

Source: IBEF report on cement industry - July 2019

- The method used for such basic demand analysis is secondary research from industry research reports. However, this has also been confirmed from individual management commentary.
- Sources used include media sources, CRISIL, CARE ratings and Ultratech Cement AR.
- **So, we can conclude that the cement industry has a supply and capacity outlook that is in line with demand growth. A major oversupply scenario is unlikely.**

Capacity Utilisation

Once the demand and supply scenarios have been understood separately, their net impact must be studied by analysing capacity utilisation levels across the industry. Whether an industry has a favourable or unfavourable demand-supply scenario, it is reflected in the capacity utilisation levels. Capacity utilisation level also plays key role in determining the profitability of a firm and an industry due to its operating leverage. Once capacity is installed, the fixed costs are determined. Now, as greater percentage of capacity is used, the fixed costs are spread over a larger base. Thus, fixed cost per unit goes down, increasing profitability. The reverse is also true. Capacity utilisation is measured in percentage terms; it is the current production out of the total possible production, if full capacity is being utilised. Capacity utilisation is neither a lagging indicator nor a leading indicator but it is a concurrent indicator of the firm's profitability.

Based on the capacity utilisation levels, an industry can be said to have overcapacity as well as undercapacity. This can be seasonal as well as structural. Seasonal undercapacity and overcapacity determine an industry's profitability for any given year. However, long-term profitability is determined by structural factors. Analysts and practitioners may want to operate in an industry with undercapacity, as that would mean superior profitability. However, they need to be on the constant lookout for new entries in the industry, entry barriers, lead time etc. New supply being created in the industry can reduce profitability.

Industries that work with overcapacity are more complicated to operate, as most firms in the industry could be operating unprofitably.

Some of the problems associated with overcapacity that can be used to identify it:

- Unsold goods

- Unfair trading practices

- Wage cuts or unemployment

- Reduced profits to collapse of the entire company

Another observation in industries with overcapacity is the need to reduce prices, thus forcing the industries into cost reduction. Such cost reduction is often at the customer's expense—feature failure, quality slippage, fewer product features etc. It also leads to distribution conflicts, wherein manufacturers seek to shift their margin pressure away from themselves on to their channels of distribution.[10] These changes in value proposition and price cuts create a space for market share shifts within the industry. These shifts are from high-priced to low-priced competitors and from less reliable competitors to more reliable competitors. Over time, the industry goes through several waves of consolidation and shakeout, wherein newer and stronger firms emerge and weaker ones are absorbed. For example, when Jio entered the telecom industry, it led to overcapacity in the industry. It forced other companies in the industry into cost reduction activities to maintain their customer base. The changes in value propositions created space for market share shifts in the industry. After waves of consolidation, weaker companies were absorbed by larger ones and newer and stronger firms emerged.[10]

Analysts and researchers must be careful while dealing with industries with oversupply as only strong players will survive and the weak ones will die, unlike industries with undersupply, where almost all the firms benefit. Oversupply is a challenge for weak firms. However, it can also be an opportunity for the stronger ones. One critical area to be reviewed is this: how long is the industry expected to stay in a state of oversupply? For industries with high exit barriers, such times can be tough and challenging for all firms. Based on capacity utilisation and undersupply/oversupply, firms would have to strategise the way forward for them.

---

[10] http://www.strategystreet.com/blog/causes_and_symptoms_of_overcapacity

CAPACITY UTILISATION ANALYSIS FOR INDIAN CEMENT INDUSTRY

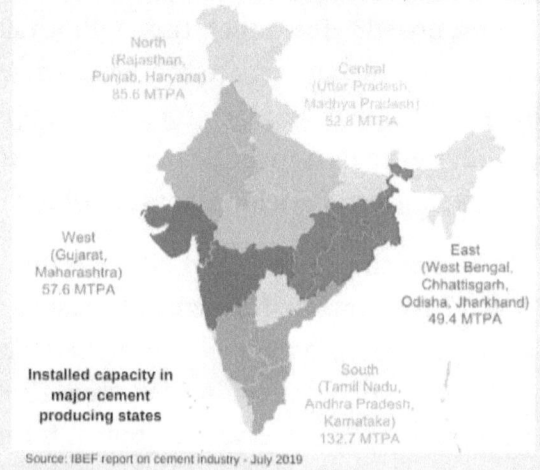

North
(Rajasthan,
Punjab, Haryana)
85.6 MTPA

Central
(Uttar Pradesh,
Madhya Pradesh)
52.8 MTPA

West
(Gujarat,
Maharashtra)
57.6 MTPA

East
(West Bengal,
Chhattisgarh,
Odisha, Jharkhand)
49.4 MTPA

Installed capacity in
major cement
producing states

South
(Tamil Nadu,
Andhra Pradesh,
Karnataka)
132.7 MTPA

- Current installed capacity (approx. as in July 2019) - 500 mtpa
- Current production - 337 mtpa
- Capacity utilisation - 71%

Source: IBEF report on cement industry - July 2019

- Going ahead, production capacity is expected to increase by 15-20 mtpa each year over the next two years.
- Demand shall increase at a pace faster than that and, therefore, capacity utilization shall go up.
- **So, we can conclude that in the cement industry, capacity utilisation can be expected to improve slightly over the medium term.**

Supply Strategies

Firms can alter the industry supply collectively based on the decisions they make. The sum of individual strategies going ahead determines the industry supply. For situations of undersupply, the incentive is to increase supply by capacity addition. The decision firms have to take is: whether to participate in the capacity expansion or not.

Expansion often involves use of resources and leverage to benefit from increased profitability due to undersupply. The underlying assumption is that the profitability will sustain and not fall going forward. However, as new supply comes up, the industry is no longer in a state of undersupply, and profitability reduces. This leaves the firm in a weak spot, as, with increased leverage and reduced profitability, the firm finds it difficult to operate efficiently going forward. Here, the analyst should focus on the demand-supply gap in quantity terms. How much new capex is being proposed? How much time will it take for new capacity to come up? Based on the answers to these questions, the analyst should decide how much time it will take for undersupply to go away. Based on this decision, the analyst must strategise whether to participate or stay away from expansion when all others are doing it.

Situations of oversupply can be a challenge as well as an opportunity for firms in an industry. Firms that have expanded capacity at a fast pace see their profitability reduce and find their balance sheets stretched with leveraged assets. Such firms find oversupply challenging. Whereas firms that had resisted capacity expansion with a conservative approach find their balance sheets to be strong and they are able to navigate through tough times in the industry. An opportunity arises for them when the weak companies go bankrupt or wish to exit the industry and sell assets at cheap prices. The stronger ones get an opportunity to consolidate operations at cheap prices and they emerge stronger when oversupply corrects itself. Analysts and practitioners thus need to strategise appropriately about when to increase supply and when not to, so that their firms are best placed to benefit when the opportunity arises.

DEMAND-SUPPLY SCENARIO FOR INDIAN CEMENT INDUSTRY- CONCLUSION

- Demand growth outlook for cement industry is stable and steady.
- There is no erratic or abrupt capacity expansion planned going forward.
- As a result, capacity utilisation is expected to improve going forward over medium term.
- There can, however, be cyclical or short-term factors that affect the demand-supply scenario in the short term. But, in the medium term and long term, the balance seems to be stable.

- **So, we can conclude that companies in the cement industry shall enjoyed increased profitability over the medium term. The structural outlook for long term too looks stable.**

(Even such basic analysis and constant updates help the investor and business manager recognise structural changes in the demand-supply scenario.
Any level of details can be examined. For more detailed research, much more emphasis should be put over the individual factors that affect demand and supply.)

Paper Industry Demand-Supply Scenario

Demand expectation
- Current industry demand (2019) - 17 mtpa
- Expected growth going forward - 7-8% p.a.
- Expected industry size 2024-25 - 23.5 mtpa

Supply scenario
- Current industry production capacity (2019) - 15 mtpa
- Expected production capacity 2024-25 - 22 mtpa

Going forward, the paper industry can expect a similar balance between demand and supply. The profitability might change in a cyclical manner but it shall be stable in the long term.

For a more detailed analysis, factors affecting the demand and supply can be evaluated individually.

Source: Indian Paper Manufacturer's Association

Impact of Overcapacity - Indian Automobile Industry 2018-19

Industry scenario
- In 2018-19, the Indian automobile sector went through a deep recession. This was mainly due to poor demand and lack of financiers due to an NBFC crisis in the country.
- Y-o-Y monthly sales had fallen by upto 30% for companies.

Signs to spot oversupply in industry
- Distribution channels filled with inventory
- Deep discounts being offered to customers
- All players in value chain - auto ancillaries, tyre manufacturers etc - negative about outlook

Impact of the slowdown on the industry
- Companies did not initially reduce production. But once inventory had piled up, capacity utilisation had to come down.
- Fixed costs continued.
- Also, prices fell as discounts were offered.
- Automobile companies faced significant drop in profits in the short run. Even though the structural outlook remained the same, the companies were struggling in the short term and medium term.

Second Tier

Once the macro scenario of the industry is understood, the value chain identified, and the industry map and profit pool identified, the second tier of the broad industry analysis comes into the picture. It emphasises the relatively more objective components of industry analysis. It focusses on identifying aspects such as market size, industry share stability, pricing power, and government regulations. This helps the analyst understand the environment in which the firm operates.

#Market Size Study

The market size of an industry is the total size of the market (in value terms or volume terms) of the customers who actually buy the industry's product or service in a given period of time. It is the total revenue or sale, in volume terms, of all the players in the industry. Identifying market size, which is also called industry size in this case, is part of the broader industry analysis. It helps understand the attractiveness of an industry by identifying the size of the opportunity. Market size can be identified by three elements.

Market size = Population x Adoption Ratio x Penetration Ratio

Population refers to the total number of people within the geographical boundaries, which define the scope of the industry. The population is the total number of people, and each person can be a potential customer to the industry. However, not all products are needed by every person. The relevant set of customers out of the total population is determined by the adoption ratio. Adoption ratio refers to the number of people out of the total population who have adapted to a particular product and its use, as they are seeking some gains and pains to be relieved. A large adoption ratio means the product is needed by a majority of the population. It is a mass-market item. Whereas a low ratio means the product is not needed by the general population, at least at that moment. While this is certainly a challenge, it can also be viewed as an opportunity. If more people adopt (to the product) going forward, it will lead to a potential growth in the industry size. However, if people do not adapt, it reduces the market size and thus the size of the opportunity.

Then comes penetration ratio. It refers to the percentage of potential customers who are currently being serviced by the players of the industry. Despite a section of the population being potential customers, an industry may not be able to service them due to barriers such as distribution challenges. This leads to low penetration of the industry. However, low penetration ratio is an opportunity as the industry can potentially grow—by working on the challenges, whereas a high ratio limits the growth through penetration. So, we can see that an industry can grow with a growing population, with more people adapting to the product/service and the industry's ability to service more of its demand.

Another potential source of growth in the industry is the formalisation of the industry. It is seen that a part of the industry is served by the organised sector and the rest is served by the unorganised sector. The unorganised share is marked by fragmented structure, poor efficiency, and lack of scale. Thus, it stands at a relative disadvantage to the organised competitors. Hence, there has been a gradual shift from the unorganised sector to the organised players in many industries This shift is evident in industries such as paint, apparel industry and footwear. Industries with a high share of unorganised players have an advantage for growth vis-à-vis the organised industry due to the migration from unorganised to organised.

Estimating Market Size

Estimating market size is by no means an exact science. Different surveys and different players identify different sizes for the same industry based on the factors they use to determine the scope of the industry. However, we can get close to the reality by following a generalised approach.

The first step for determining the size of the industry is determining the boundaries of the industry— activity-wise and geography-wise. This is then followed by determining a time horizon i.e. monthly, annual or even for a longer horizon. Following this, a population estimate for the geographical area is established. Once the population is known, a sample survey is conducted to know the adoption rate and the penetration rate. These ratios are multiplied with the population size to estimate the industry size. This gives a primary estimate of the industry size.

The process of identifying the primary estimate for industry size can be time-taking, expensive and not very rewarding for the amount of effort spent. Thus, secondary estimates for industry sizes may be used. These include government data, trade association data and financial data from major players. Information from these sources help estimate the industry size.

Hair Oil Market in India

Hair oil market in India	2007	2010	2015	2019	2025E
Total market size (in Rs.)	2827 cr	5044 cr	9390 cr	13168 cr	20000 cr
Organised market share	40%			65%	
Unorganised market share	60%			35%	

*Source: Bajaj Consumer Care Ltd Annual Reports

- Market size data is obtained through a secondary source i.e. a company disclosure. Data regarding evolution of industry size and shift from unorganised to organised sector is obtained.
- It can be observed that the industry has grown at a decent pace. Going ahead as well, the industry outlook seems good. How big a company in the industry can become is determined by the industry size.

The major purpose of an industry size analysis for analysts as well as practitioners is to identify the potential size of the opportunity and the potential growth going forward. The industry size trend is observed over time in an attempt to get hints for the future; also, the industry size is broken down to smaller elements so that the potential of growth can be identified. It is possible for industries to stay stable in volume terms but grow in value terms. Market size analysis becomes particularly important when analysing bigger companies in an industry, as their growth is closely linked with industry growth. Industry size analysis is not very important in the context of smaller companies as their growth depends much more on company-specific factors rather than industry growth. A growing industry, however, makes it easier for all players—big or small—to grow at a decent pace.

Technical Textiles Market in India

Technical textiles market in India	2008	2013	2018	2021E
Total market size (in Rs.)	36775 cr	65920 cr	116217 cr	200823 cr
Organised market share	90%		85%	
Unorganised market share	10%		15%	

- It is seen that the industry has been growing at a decent pace and the size of opportunity is relatively high.
- Any firm that is able to scale successfully in technical textiles can become huge. However, the firm would have to operate across sub segments.

#Industry Stability

Industry stability determines how quickly players in the industry gain and lose market share. This metric of market share is used to get a general idea about the size of a company in relation to its market and its competitors. This is an indicator of relative competitiveness or strength of the company's products and services.

Industries in which companies gain and lose market share quickly are relatively less stable than industries where companies take time to do so. In less stable industries, entry and scaling up can be relatively quicker and easier, but benefitting from gained market share and maintaining it over time can be very difficult. In more stable industries, entry can take time and can be very difficult, but once market share is gained, it can be maintained for a while and the firms can benefit from their position.

There are many factors that determine the stability of any industry. They are discussed in the following paragraphs.

Constant Product Innovation

Constant product innovation by companies in the industry leads to companies coming up with products that exceed the offerings of the previous best product in the market. This causes market share to shift towards the firm with the new offering. This will later shift to another firm that comes up with an even better offering. When this happens at a fast pace, it leads to instability in the industry, in terms of market share.

New Business Models

New business models constantly coming up in the industry leads to disruptive forces in the industry. Hence, established firms lose market share to newer firms. New business models make the older ones obsolete, thus causing changes in market share. Another common factor is the ease of financing available around the industry. Industries that are 'hot' and 'favourite' currently attract a lot of new capital. Large amounts of capital for new firms allow them to do things at scale, thus taking away the advantage of scale of existing firms. This causes some shift in the market share from existing to new firms.

Lowering of Entry Barriers and Switching Costs

Industries facing value migration see new winners emerging and established players losing market share. Two factors that contribute to this and reduce industry stability are lowering of entry barriers and lowering of switching costs. As entry barriers reduce, new firms with innovative value propositions and business models can join the industry and challenge the established players in the industry. Also lowering of switching costs for the customers can allow them to look for competitors' products, thus causing shifts in the market share in the industry.

Government Regulations

Another factor that contributes to industry instability is the impact of government regulations. Government regulations can overnight take away the advantages of established players and create space for new firms to join the industry and rapidly gain market share. Constant regulatory changes cause firms to gain and lose market share quickly, thus making the industry unstable.

Business Cycle

The last contributing factor is business cycle. This is particularly the case with commodity industries and industries with a relatively short business cycle. During periods of expansion of the industry, new players join the industry and existing ones increase capacity and gain market share. However, during periods of downturn, only the strong companies are able to survive whereas those with a stretched balance sheet fail to survive and they are bought over by the existing firms. Thus, severe market share shifts occur over various stages of the business cycle.

Understanding industry stability is important for both the entrepreneur as well as the investor. It is easier to enter and gain market share in industries with instability in market share, such as the mobile phone industry. However, it is difficult to maintain the market share in these industries. Thus, the entrepreneur and investor must know the degree of stability in their industry as it will determine the longevity of returns for them. In other words, industry stability determines the balance between pace of growth and longevity of returns.

Industry Stability - Indian Smartphone Players

	FY2014	FY2016	FY2019
Micromax	21%	13 %	1.1%
Intex	1%	12%	0.1%
Lava	8%	6%	1.2%
Karbonn	9.6%	4%	0.2%
Xiaomi	-	9%	29%
Vivo	-	1%	12%
Realme	-	-	7%
oppo	-	3%	7%
Samsung	25%	24%	23%

*Source: Media Outlets

We see that the market share of these companies is changing quickly. Thus, the industry can be counted as an unstable one, prone to quick market share shifts.

Industry Stability - Indian Paints Industry

Company	2010	2015	2019
Asian Paints	59.4%	57.5%	57%
Berger Paints	16.9%	17.6%	18.6%
Kansai Nerolac	15.3%	14.6%	15.34%
Akzo Nobel	8.2%	10.39%	8.65%
Total	100%	100%	100%

- The market share of top 4 players is studied to understand the industry stability in terms of market share.
- We see that the top 4 players (which form 70% of the market) have hardly moved over 10 years.
- So, we can conclude that it is a very stable industry and it is difficult to gain and lose market share.

Pricing Power in the Industry

The pricing power of any firm is its ability to increase the market price of the goods or services that it offers, over and above the increase in the raw material prices. Pricing power is dependent on supply and demand for the product from the customer.

A company or industry does not have much pricing power if an increase in prices would lessen the demand for their products. This phenomenon is captured in the price elasticity of demand. Price elasticity of demand is the degree to which consumers change their demand in quantity terms in response to changes in the price of the product. Also, a company or industry does not have much pricing power if an increase in prices can cause new entrants to the industry and increase supply in the industry. This phenomenon is captured in price elasticity of supply. Price elasticity of supply is the degree to which producers can change their supply in volume terms in response to changes in the price of the product.[11]

Industries in which the price elasticity of demand as well as price elasticity of supply are low have the highest pricing power. Here, neither does new supply come in when prices rise nor do the consumers reduce their demand. Industries in which either the demand or supply (or both) is elastic, firms find it difficult to have a high pricing power.

There are several factors that influence price elasticity of demand and supply. These should be assessed to determine the industries with a high pricing power.

Factors That Affect Price Elasticity of Demand

- **Number of close substitutes:** If a product has a number of close substitutes, it leads to consumers switching between the substitutes in response to price changes. Thus, the product has a high price elasticity. Such products find it difficult to have pricing power. For example, air travel has no close substitute for inter-continental travel but trains and cars are close substitutes for journeys around 200–400 km between major cities in a large country.

- **Cost of switching:** Switching costs determine the ease with which consumers can switch between products. Higher the switching costs, more inelastic is the demand. Switching costs include financial cost, psychological cost, hassle, and technical training. For instance, a person trained in one accounting

---

[11]   https://www.investopedia.com/terms/p/pricingpower.asp

software may not switch to another as he would need to retrain himself in the new software. This acts as a switching cost.

- **Degree of necessity:** Necessities tend to have an inelastic demand whereas goods that are luxuries are more elastic in demand. For instance, prices for basic pulses, fruits and grains remain inelastic whereas the prices of fancy clothes and mobile phones are relatively elastic.

- **Proportion of income allocated to spending on product:** If a product forms a large proportion of total spending by the consumer, the consumer tends to be more concerned about the product and thus the price is more elastic. At the same time, for items that form a small percentage of total consumption, the demand is inelastic. For example, the demand for a car is price elastic. However, when buying ball bearings, a small part in the car, the demand is inelastic.

- **Whether the good is subject to habitual consumption:** Some products become habits for the consumer and their consumption becomes less price elastic. It becomes a default choice. For example, cigarettes and liquor.

Products that have low price elasticity of demand do not see consumers moving away in response to increases in prices. These products have a relatively higher pricing power. Also, price elasticity of supply must be understood.

Major Factors That Influence Price Elasticity of Supply

- **Ability to store output:** Goods that can be safely stored have a relatively elastic supply over perishable goods that cannot be stored for long. For instance, consumer durables can be stored and have an elastic supply, whereas fruits and vegetables cannot be stored for long.

- **Factor mobility:** If the factors of production can be moved easily from one use to another and are not industry-specific, they will affect the elasticity of supply. Higher the mobility of the factors, more elastic is the supply. For example, if a job does not require any specific skill-set, the labour from other industries can move to this industry, in periods of high production requirements when the industry's services are in overdemand.

- **Changes in cost of production:** With expansion of output, if the cost of production increases and the profitability falls, producers would not increase supply, thus making supply less elastic.

- **Availability of resources:** One of the most important factors to increase supply is the availability of adequate resources. If land, labour, capital and technology are adequately available, with ease, the supply will be elastic.

Price elasticity of demand and supply together determine the changes in demand and supply in response to the price of the product, thus determining the pricing power of the product. However, there are a few other factors that also contribute to determining the pricing power in any industry.

Other Factors That Determine Pricing Power

- **Product differentiation:** If a player in an industry can provide differentiated products and services that are needed by a particular customer segment, the firm will gain pricing power as there is no close substitute available. For instance, a pharmaceutical company developing a drug after years of research and development will have immense pricing power.

- **Brand power:** Products that are backed by powerful brands have an ability to charge the customer a premium. These brands give them pricing power over similar substitutes. For example, Maggi noodles and Parle-G biscuits allow the companies Nestle and Parle Products to charge a premium.

- **Regulatory factors:** Regulatory factors can both increase as well as decrease pricing power within any industry. They can limit the entry into any industry and thus reduce price elasticity of supply. They can also enable existing players to increase their prices and enjoy increased profitability.

At the same time, some industries have their prices regulated. In such cases, despite the companies having the market power to increase prices, they are not able to do so. This leads to poor pricing power. For instance, many pharmaceutical drugs have their prices regulated, thus leaving no pricing power with such companies.

Based on the factors discussed above, the pricing power of various players in the industry is ascertained. Entrepreneurs and analysts must look for industries that command a higher pricing power. However, it is difficult to enter such industries. But once entry is established, the players can be highly profitable.

Pricing Power - Colgate Palmolive (India) Ltd

(in Rs. unless otherwise stated)

	FY2015	FY2016	FY2017	FY2018	FY2019
Revenue	3981 cr	3868 cr	3981 cr	4187 cr	4462 cr
Direct Costs	2027 cr	2150 cr	2183 cr	2225 cr	2321 cr
Gross Profit Margin (%)	49.08%	44.42 %	45.16 %	46.86 %	47.98 %

- So, it is seen that Colgate India can increase prices over and above increase in raw material prices without impacting its sales.
- Gross profit margins can be used as an indicator to check pricing power in any industry. If GPM can be increased with ease, the industry or firm has price power.

#Competitive Life Cycle

Just like a person who is born, grows, matures, eventually declines, and ultimately experiences death, industries and product lines too go through such a life cycle. New, unique product offerings are developed by new firms or even existing ones. Thus, a new industry begins. This industry then takes time to prove its concept to a small group of customers, before it is adopted by the masses. Over time, new competitors join the industry. Finally the industry degrows with falling profitability. The growth of an industry's sales over time is used to chart its life cycle. Different stages in the industry's life cycle are identified based on the behaviour of the sales.

For instance, when tablets were introduced, they were met with lot of fanfare and they found success. Now the sales of tablets have stabilised. There is only linear growth and no exponential growth, thus marking a mature stage.

Knowing which stage of the life cycle the industry is in is important for both the entrepreneur as well the investor. Each stage has different characteristics in terms of how profits, revenue and assets behave and the number of competitors in the market. Based on the stage and its characteristics, the business strategy differs. Also for investors, the amount of cash required by the business and the returns that they can expect vary significantly based on the life cycle stage the industry is in.

The different stages of the industry's competitive life cycle and strategies that are most suitable for various stages are discussed ahead. The key is to correctly identify the current stage of the industry and determine what the entrepreneur or investor should expect in terms of the behaviour of the companies going forward.

#Innovation

The first stage is when a new and unique offering has been developed by a small entrepreneurial company or even a proven company, which develops something new through its research and development efforts. This marks the beginning of a new industry. The innovation can come in various forms—it may be a product that opens up an entirely new market, replaces an existing product, or significantly broadens the market for an existing product.[12]

When such a new product is brought to the market, customer demand is limited due to unfamiliarity with the product's features and performance. Distribution channels and the relevant supporting infrastructure are still underdeveloped;[13] for example, charging ecosystem for electric vehicles. The complementary goods required for use of the product are not adequately available. Marketing strategies during this stage are intended to explain the product and its

---

[12]   https://www.slideshare.net/ashishKPD/product-life-cycle-26664029
[13]   https://corporatefinanceinstitute.com/resources/knowledge/strategy/
       industry-life-cycle/

uses to the consumers and thus create awareness for the product and the industry.[14]

At the introduction stage, the product's use and market are not proven. Thus, only the early adopters are trying the product at this stage. As a result, sales are low and slow. Also, per-unit costs of manufacturing are high. Thus, low profits and heavy cash investments mark this stage.

The major characteristics of this stage are:

- Low and slow sales

- High product price

- Heavy promotional expense

- Lack of knowledge

- Low profits

- Narrow product lines[12]

At this stage, firms should focus on advertising that is informative to the potential buyers. As the product is new, firms should not hold back on heavy advertising and promotional expenses. The firms should also focus on selective distribution and segments where they can find early adopters.

[12]   https://www.slideshare.net/ashishKPD/product-life-cycle-26664029
[14]   https://pt.scribd.com/document/67260150/stm

Autonomous Cars Industry - Industry in Innovation Phase

Companies across the globe are working on developing and innovating various models of autonomous cars. A variety of Indian startups are working on the same.

- **Hi Tech Robotic Systemz** - Gurgaon-based startup that developed Novus Drive - a completely autonomous EV

- **ATI motors** - Bangalore-based company that is designing electric cargo vehicles

- **Auro Robotics** - Developed self-driving shuttle, being run in University of Santa Clara

- **Fisheybox** - Kolkata-based startup that has an autonomous Celerio that can be run by a joystick

Various other companies are working on products with varying degrees of success. A lot of Japanese, American and Chinese players are also working on the same. Japan is set to test the success of these vehicles as soon as the 2020 Tokyo Olympics.

Characteristics of the industry

- Lack of knowledge among customers
- Low and slow sales
- Proof of concept not yet established
- High prices
- Narrow product lines

The above features of the industry help us to identify the industry as one in the innovation phase.

#Growth

Only if a new product satisfies the needs of a market, it will enter the growth stage, wherein new customers come and sales increase at a fast pace. As a bigger market segment is attracted towards the product, new companies also join the industry. This causes a fall in prices. However, as production volume increases, cost per unit also falls, and thus profitability starts to rise. As the product price goes down, customer demand increases. Here, complementary products are also available in the market; so people have greater benefits purchasing the product and its components.

Major characteristics of the growth stage are:

- Rapid increase in sales

- Product improvements

- Increase in competition

- Increase in profits

- Reduction in price

- Strengthening the distribution channel[12]

At this stage, firms should focus on improving product quality, features and performance. They may enter new market areas. New versions and models at different price points should be introduced in order to cater to the requirements of different types of buyers. Firms should focus on brand image creation of the product through promotional activities.

The growth stage may be longer due to frequent product upgrades and enhancements that forestall movement into maturity.[15] If product innovation has not kept pace with competing products and services or

[12]   https://www.slideshare.net/ashishKPD/product-life-cycle-26664029
[15]   http://www.ialc.org/file/documents/workshops/2015-rouen/Industry_
       lifecycle_seminar_handout.pdf

if new innovations and technological changes have caused the industry to become obsolete, sales will suffer and the life cycle will experience a phase of decline.[16]

Ed Tech industry in India - An Industry in Growth stage

- A lot of Indian ed tech companies have been gaining attraction in the recent past.
- Companies like BYJU's, Unacademy and upGrad have been finding acceptance in the market and have been effectively replacing traditional modes of education.
- Tech-enabled education firms have been accepted by the Indian parents and have picked up in the last few years.

Characteristics of the industry

- Rapid increase in sales
- Product improvements and product line expansion
- Increase in competition
- Increase in profits for the companies
- Reduction in price of the product
- Focus on distribution channel expansion

Due to the above characteristics of the industry, the industry can be identified as a growth industry.

---

[16] https://www.encyclopedia.com/entrepreneurs/encyclopedias-almanacs-transcripts-and-maps/industry-life-cycle

#Maturity

At the maturity stage, revenue growth, cash flows and profit start slowing down. At this stage, companies realise maximum revenue, profits and cashflows because customer demand is fairly high and consistent. A majority of the companies in the industry are well-established, and the industry reaches its saturation point. Some firms are naturally eliminated as they are unable to grow along with the industry, thus still generating negative cash flows. Companies at this stage collectively attempt to moderate the intensity of competition to protect themselves and maintain profitability.[17]

Firms continue to focus on differentiating their offerings from that of industry competitors. Innovations continue in the industry. But they are not as radical as before and may only be slight changes or cosmetic improvements in colour or formulation to stress on the 'new' and 'improved' aspect to consumers.

The major characteristics of the stage are:

- Sales increases at decreasing rate

- Normal promotional expenses

- Uniform and lower prices

- Product modifications

- Dealer support

- Profit margin decreases[12]

Here, firms must focus on improving the quality of the product and introduce new models. They must also focus on increasing usage among current customers and pursue the development of new uses

[17]   https://corporatefinanceinstitute.com/resources/knowledge/strategy/industry-life-cycle/

[12]   https://www.slideshare.net/ashishKPD/product-life-cycle-26664029

of the product. They must try to convert non-users into users of the product. These are some of the common strategies used by industries entering maturity phase.

#Decline

The final stage is when sales eventually begin to fall under the impact of new product competition and changing consumer behaviour. The sales and profits fall down sharply and, as a result, promotional expenditure has to be cut down drastically. To deal with the decline, companies may choose to focus on their most profitable product lines or services in order to maximise profits and stay in the industry. Some large companies focus on acquiring smaller or failing competitors to become the dominant player.[18]

The common features of industries that are in the decline stage are:

- Rapid decrease in sales

- Further decrease in prices

- No or very little promotional expenses

- Suspension of production work

The competitive life cycle discussed earlier denotes the stages an industry passes through at different speeds in the course of completing the whole cycle. It can be seen that no two industries have identical life cycles. The duration for each stage is different for different products. It is not necessary that all products go through all the stages; some fail at the initial stage, while others may reach the decline stage directly, skipping the maturity stage. Also, when an industry moves from one stage to another, the transition occurs over a period of time. It becomes

[18]   https://corporatefinanceinstitute.com/resources/knowledge/strategy/
        industry-life-cycle/

difficult for analysts to correctly identify the stage the industry is in. So, analysts must be careful while identifying such periods of transition.

The life cycle of an industry depends on various factors:

- Rate of technological change

- Rate of market acceptance

- Competitor's entry

- Economic and managerial forces

- Risk-bearing capacity

- Government policy[19]

Even within the same industry, various firms may be at different life cycle stages. This is because some firms are able to find new uses for their declining products, thus extending their life cycle. Firms have a varying ability to prolong their life cycle based on their strategic choices.[20]

Some of the common strategies to extend product life cycle are:

- Product modification

- Entry into a new market

- Promoting frequent use

- Developing different usage

- Use of aggressive advertising and sales promotion techniques[19]

Entrepreneurs and investors must know the stage the industry is in before entering it, so as to know what behaviour of revenues, cash and profits can be expected from the industry and its firms. Once the

[19]   https://www.slideshare.net/ashishKPD/product-life-cycle-26664029
[20]   https://pt.scribd.com/document/67260150/stm

stage of cycle has been identified, it is important to be on the lookout for any disruptions that might affect the industry. Disruptions affect the industry, irrespective of the stage the industry is in, and are thus constant threats as well as opportunities for all industries.

Handicraft Industry in India - An Industry in Decline Stage

- Indian handicrafts have been losing market to machinery manufactured fabrics for a few decades now.
- The industry finds it difficult to compete in terms of manufacturing cost to mass manufactured textiles.
- Even though the quality and art in handicrafts is considered superior, customers prefer the cheaper mass manufactured product.
- As a result, the industry has been squeezing with falling profitability.

Characteristics of the industry

- Decrease in prices
- Decrease in volumes and sales
- Low expenses on promotions
- Suspension of production related work
- Distribution channels refusing to stock inventory and give display space to the industry
- Old practioners are exiting the industry

Due to the above characteristics of the industry, the industry can be identified as an industry in decline phase.

Disruptions

Industry disruption is a topic that interests all firms, big and small alike, as it allows a smaller firm in the industry or even a start-up with fewer resources to successfully challenge the established incumbent businesses. However, disruption is one of the most misused words in business literature. Anything that is slightly different from status quo and is able to make its mark is said to be 'disruptive' in nature. Anything that slightly modifies the current market or enhances the value proposition is considered to be 'disruptive'. For instance, finding new modes of distribution or adding new features to the product is often said to be a disruption.

In reality, disruption is something that is much rarer and more difficult to execute. True disruption happens when something displaces something else to create something very new. Harvard Business School professor and disruption guru Clayton Christensen says that a disruption displaces an existing market, industry or technology and produces something that is new, more efficient and worthwhile. It is at once destructive as well as creative.

The risk of industry disruptions is one of the most significant risks that worry managers and investors of established companies. This is primarily because, as a consequence of being disrupted, the firm's product or business model may become obsolete and lose market to disruptive forces. Today, most industries face the risk of disruption due to new external factors gaining in prominence.

Some of these forces that affect all businesses are:

–   New business models that bring around new competitive dynamics to existing firms where what was an advantage for them turns into a disadvantage. For example, assets for hotel companies and car rental companies are obstructions to them in scaling up. New business models that involve partnering instead of owning these assets have emerged and they have been able to scale very quickly. New revenue models such as pay-per-use and subscription models are disrupting many industries.

– Regulatory changes have the ability to completely change the dynamics of an industry, shifting from one set of players and creating space for new players.

– Forces of technology have allowed centralisation of some industries, at the same time democratising some. This has completely changed the competitive dynamics of many industries.

Understanding disruption, disruptive forces and threat of disruption is of utmost importance for both entrepreneurs as well as analysts. They are expected to anticipate, respond to and thrive in the face of disruption. They are expected to keep their firm, its business model and its people flexible enough so that they benefit in case of any disruptive force rather than stand at a position of disadvantage due to their rigidity. However, this is easier said than done, as companies are continuously faced by challengers. In the beginning, almost all challengers look like the previous ones that had failed. But only after they have gained scale do the incumbent firms realise the threat to their business.

Managers at the incumbent firms are often doubtful that the market for disruption exists and the challenger's business model is viable. Most of them are sceptical that innovation and disruption will take place. They adopt a wait-and-see approach to the new market. As the challenger grows and it becomes clearer that the business model is viable, incumbents start creating contingency plans. At the core of the responses is a belief in the 'fast-follower' strategy. However, when competing on a new plane of competition, the resources and experiences the incumbents have developed in their original model are unlikely to help them and may even hurt them. Thus, identifying and responding to challenges is not an easy task but one of the most important factors that should be in the radar of entrepreneurs and investors.[21]

Innovations and disruptions can be of different kinds, each differing in the intensity of the consequences it has on the established firms in the industry and the best strategy to respond to them. These are sustaining innovations, low-end innovations (disruptive) and new market innovations (disruptive).

#Sustaining Innovation

A sustaining innovation improves existing products. It does not create new markets or destroy existing markets but enhances existing ones with a better value proposition.[21] Sustaining innovation is done within the same value chain that the industry works on. It leads to better products, advanced technology and better raw materials. Sustaining innovation is the way firms within an industry compete.

Some sustaining innovations are incremental year-by-year improvements, which all good companies grind out. Other sustaining innovations are breakthrough innovations, wherein the product leapfrogs beyond the competition's products.[22] It does not matter how technologically difficult the innovation is, it is almost always that established competitors win the battles of sustaining innovations from the challengers. Sustaining innovation is not disruptive in nature and does not change the plane of competition.

The best strategy for firms to respond to such sustaining innovations is to participate in this innovative process or change as it is generally a one-way street. Those who do not change as per the changing consumer needs are often left behind, and over time they lose market share.

[21]   https://medium.com/@tom_bartman/confronting-a-new-market-disruption-when-disrupting-the-disruptor-is-the-only-way-to-succeed-f02355ad919b
[22]   http://www.slideshare.net/prateekjaiswal/3a-new-product-development

The firms should try and be the pioneers of these innovative changes through research and development efforts. However, those left behind should follow a 'fast-follower' approach.

Amazon Kindle - A Sustaining Innovation

- Books have been printed for centuries. They were expensive and difficult to find.
- Then came e-readers like Kindle that provided a similar experience, but was much cheaper.
- The books could simply be bought and downloaded.

E-reader makes the book cheap and more accessible. It is a sustaining innovation that complements paperback books. Traditional publishers now publish all books in an e-book version.

#Low-end Innovation (Disruptive)

Low-end innovation happens when a new value chain is created by offering a product that already exists at a cheaper, easier-to-use manner, thus attracting the least-demanding customers of the already existing industry towards it. The companies adopt a new operating or financial approach and use these low-cost business models that pick from the least attractive customers of established firms.

Low-end innovations are disruptive in nature as they have the ability to create, over time, new markets that are distinct from the mainstream market and displace them as more and more people switch. Initially, large and established firms focus on improving their products and services for their most demanding customers and usually most profitable customer segments. In doing this, they exceed the needs of some segments and ignore the needs of others. Entrants or challengers that prove to be disruptive begin by successfully targeting those overlooked segments, thus gaining foothold by delivering more suitable value propositions, often at a lower price.[23]

The most ideal strategy here is for the company to respond to entrants in the low end of the market. This is, however, not that easy as it becomes very difficult to identify successful challengers as everyone looks similar at the start. However, keeping the entry doors closed through the low-end market is an essential activity that managers should keep in mind. Otherwise, a successful disruptor can take away their market share.

Tata Nano - A Low-End Disruption

- To make cars more affordable and accessible, Tata Motors in India created Nano.
- It made cars more accessible by removing many extra features.
- The car created immense functional utility.
- However, the car failed in creating social utility. It was looked down upon.

However, the concept of Nano was a low-end disruption that allowed many to give up two-wheelers and become first-time car owners.

---

[23]   https://medium.com/@imnotjk/the-end-of-disruption-ab11fffa34fd

Virtual Schools - A Low-End Disruption

- Traditional schools have been providing a lot of benefits - one-on-one attention and supervision.
- However, not everyone needs such attention.
- Some wish to lean at their own speed and at a cheaper rate.
- This is why virtual schools and online courses have found great success.

Online courses and virtual schools have allowed many students to learn otherwise expensive skills. As a result, many offline institutions have also opened virtual training divisions.

#New Market Innovations

New market disruptions involve making a product more affordable to own or use, thus allowing a new population to experience the product. This leads to creation of a new market that is simpler to use. Here, the challenger with his value proposition is competing against 'non-consumption' of the existing product. This opens up, and expands, an all-new market for the product with the users.

There is no clear strategy on how incumbents should behave in new market disruptions. If the new market created has the potential to replace the existing one, the firm should respond either by trying to outcompete the challenger in the initial days itself or by getting involved in the new market. If the incumbent is confident that the disruption would not take away their market but only create a new one, they may choose to ignore it. However, the risk remains that the challenger may later alter the value proposition and become a direct competitor in the incumbent's industry.

Today, all industries face the risk of being disrupted with new technologies and business models coming in. All entrepreneurs and investors should see this as a challenge as well as an opportunity. The potential threats of disruption, forces of disruption and degree of competition by challengers are topics that should be understood by everyone before entering any industry.

Social Media Ads - New Market Disruption for Advertisers

- Traditional advertising was expensive and could only be done by bigger companies with huge budgets.
- Social media allows targeted ads for much less.
- It allows a completely new set of users to access the advertising market.

As social media allows an entirely new set of advertisers, it creates a new market for the media industry, disrupting what existed earlier with direct competition. As it creates new users, it is a new-market disruption.

Government Regulations About the Industry

Governments establish many regulations and policies that guide businesses. Many of these policies are specific to given industries whereas others affect businesses in general. Businesses need to be flexible enough to respond to changing rules and policies, as lack of flexibility can put firms out of business. These policies not only apply at the national level but they also apply more locally, as states and municipalities have their own set of rules. There are international treaties that influence the way business is done.

Government policies and regulations always depend on the political culture of the country and the political climate at the moment. A stable political system can make business-friendly decisions whereas an unstable system has a negative impact on the business environment.

It is very important for entrepreneurs, business managers and investors to know about policies and regulations affecting their concerned industries. Policies have the power to act as a market catalyst by changing the behaviour in the business environment. For instance, the government can underwrite the development of any particular industry by providing special incentives and devising initiatives. They can provide tax and duty exemptions on different sectors that will trigger investment and growth in that sector. Also, the government can impose more taxes and duties on any particular sector that will make investors lose their interest in that sector. The government establishes various regulatory authorities for different industries. Firms in industries have different licensing requirements and permit requirements. Anyone getting into any industry or belonging to any industry must understand the government's policies and regulations affecting them. Also, they should have an understanding about the current government's attitude towards the particular industry.

Tax: The government earns its revenues through direct and indirect taxes that affects businesses. Government agencies establish tax policies that are standard to everyone and apply to all businesses equally, irrespective of their industries. However, some industries are allowed certain special incentives whereas some others are asked to pay excess tax. The industries that the government wishes to promote, such as those that create employment or protect the environment, are allowed tax incentives. At the same time, industries that the government wishes to restrict are imposed with additional taxes so as to discourage investment.

The government agencies also decide the indirect taxes imposed on different goods. Indirect taxes are borne by the end customer and they decide the final price of the product. Lower levels of indirect taxes reduce the final price of the product, thus encouraging consumption. Also, the government provides various subsidies to select industries to promote entry in these industries. Entrepreneurs and investors must know about special taxes and subsidies affecting their industries.

Export-import duties: Not all industries involve import and export of goods and services. But those that do need to pay differing amounts of duties, for each nation that they import from or export to. The duties depend on the balance of trade and the balance of payments of the country with other nations and the government's focus on the sector.

Analysts and business managers must understand the export and import duties charged by both the countries—the source and the destination country. They should keep in mind that any change in duties or imposition of any tax can make the product less competent, causing the industry's market size to shrink or expand, based on policy changes. Analysts and managers must be aware of any international treaty involving the industry and the various permits and restrictions on foreign trade in that particular product or industry.

Foreign Tax changes and implications

US - China Trade War

- US- China Trade war since 2017 has caused both the countries to put duties on imports from goods manufactured in the other country.
- This has caused industries in both the countries suffering as the demand is affected by making them incompetent.

Indian Steel and aluminium industry

- For India, USA imposed raised import duties from 10% to 25% for steel and aluminium products which significantly impacted the industry.

Environmental laws: Most commercial activities impact the environment in a negative manner. International treaties and general public pressure force governments to make laws that limit or regulate the amount of environmental damage. For instance, many areas are identified to be no-logging zones where no wood can be cut for timber. The carbon footprint of nations and industries and the liquid discharge by industries are monitored to keep a check on the extent of environmental damage done.

Entrepreneurs and investors must know the extent of environment damage done by their industries, the industry-specific rules, and the environmental clearances required to operate. Any change in environment-related laws or violation by the companies can significantly impact their ability to continue, as permits to operate may come under threat. Also, the firms must take adequate precautionary measures to minimise the impact as much as possible.

Legal acts/provisions/notices: Governments establish special acts or provisions that mandate how an industry should behave. In more rigid forms, these acts establish regulatory agencies that regulate the industry. It is imperative for analysts to understand the various laws, acts and provisions that affect the industry. They should also keep track of the developments in the regulatory body's decisions regarding the industry. For instance, the banks in India are regulated by Reserve Bank of India; investment firms are regulated by Securities and Exchange Board of India.

Also, various industries fall under different ministries of the government. For instance, the textile industry has a separate textile ministry at the union level; defence manufacturers have to deal with the Defence ministry. Thus, analysts and business managers should keep track of developments in these ministries and also stay updated about the latest developments within the industry. Also, staying abreast of ministry websites will allow them to identify opportunities presented by the government.

Various notices by regulators and ministries help them stay updated and notify industry participants of any changes. Entrepreneurs and investors must track these notices keenly as any change can cause significant changes to their business.

Ownership related laws: A few industries are recognised to be sensitive to a country's interest. For instance, a company owning majority of the key natural resources of the country. Also, for securities exchange like BSE or NSE, where a country's securities are traded, ownership of such an exchange might give an unfair advantage to the owner. Thus, for companies and industries that are critical to a country's general interests, ownership related laws are restrictive. These limit the ability to own companies in that industry. Laws might limit the maximum percentage of the company that can be owned in an industry by an individual, thus securing diversified ownership. Laws might limit the maximum ownership allowed by foreign companies or the maximum foreign direct investment allowed in a given sector. Such restrictive practices limit the growth for industries. Analysts and entrepreneurs must know about such ownership related laws, so as to plan for them accordingly, well in time.

Ownership Related Policies

Case of single brand retail in India

- Single brand retail in India had its FDI capped for very long at 49% on the grounds of it being a threat to local farmers, small artists, small shop owners etc.
- The government, after long debates, allowed 100% FDI. It also allowed owning direct online stores before physical stores in India.
- This allowed the likes of IKEA and Walmart (through Flipkart acquisition) to enter India and had implications by changing the dynamics of various industries.

Other industry-specific regulations: There are various other industry-specific measures and regulations that need to be followed, so as to operate in the industry. For instance, many industries need their products and machines to be quality-and-standards-compliant; many industries need their premises to be compulsorily fire-compliant. Other industries may have specific labour laws. Such laws and regulations that are specific to the industry must be understood by the analysts and business managers.

Regulations - Steel Industry in India

Taxes

- GST - 18% (better than earlier 19.5% indirect taxes)
- Corporate tax reduced to 25% in 2019

Export / Import regulations

- From a controlled import regime, industry has moved to a free import regime.
- However, anti-dumping and safeguard duties are often used.
- Free export is allowed; also at times promoted.

Environmental regulations

- Covered under Environment Protection Act and Ministry of Environment and Forest
- All new plants and substantial expansions require permission under EPA
- Install specific pollution control equipment

Investment related regulations

- Until 1991, only government sector companies were allowed. In 1991, private sector was allowed.
- 100% FDI is allowed.

Other industry-specific regulations

- Pricing and distribution deregulated from January 1992
- National Steel Policy drafted in 2005 acts as basis for all government planning about the industry
- Energy consumption laws that put obsolete factories out of use
- Government pledged to reduce GHG emission by the industry by 33-35% under Intended Nationally Determined Contribution.

Recent News Related to the Industry

The importance of being educated about the latest industry updates cannot be underestimated. It does not matter what type of business it is, not keeping up to date with what is new in the industry could leave the business vulnerable to security issues or lead it to unknowingly fail to comply with new regulations. Moreover, businesses that aren't informed of the latest industry updates also risk losing out to competitors by failing to deliver consumers what they want. Staying updated is the only way in which managers can identify forthcoming changes and shifts in the industry early enough and benefit from them.[24]

Some of the common benefits of keeping an active track of the industry are:

– Industry updates and compliance with regulations

– Being aware of industry updates allows one to identify new opportunities and threats early

– Using the knowledge to understand and deliver what customers want

– Increases awareness of security issues

– Helps keep ahead of the competition

Recent news about the companies in the industry can come in various forms and from multiple sources. All forms of news that influence the business environment of the firm and the industry are of relevance to both the entrepreneur as well as the analyst. News that influences the business environment refers to news that affects the factors of the business environment. The factors include political, social, economic, technological and legal factors. Company-specific updates are as important as industry updates. They can come from strategies adopted by the management of large companies and other communication given out by them.

---

[24]   https://preferredpayments.com/importance-being-know-industry-news/

Government updates like recent circulars by regulatory bodies, updates from relevant ministries, and interviews with key people in the government are a rich source of information to stay updated about the industry. It is important to know, keep track of, and get early insights into key technological upgrades around the industry and changes in customer's tastes and preferences.

However, what remains a challenge is not just knowing the news that is relevant but also making the correct analysis of the same and having a relevant understanding of the consequences that the news will have. There is no exact way to know the correct interpretation of the news. However, the reason behind mentioning this is to draw attention to the fact that focus should not only be on knowing the appropriate news but also on getting the correct interpretation of the same. Being open to and listening to multiple interpretations and views remains one of the best defences of an entrepreneur or investor.

News and Its Implications

In a notification of Department of Economic Affairs in November 2017 infrastructure status was awarded to logistics sector

Implications:
- Shall attract more funding at competitive rates
- Now cold chain and warehouse facilities are covered in infrastructure status
- Allows insurance companies and pension funds and international lenders to fund companies in logistics space and logistics projects
- Cheaper ECB loans

The key is to not merely know the news but also know what industry-specific impact it will create and how that will impact the health of the industry in the long run.

The important sources of industry news are:

- Newspaper and TV

- YouTube channels about the industry

- Books and magazines

- Management interviews and commentary at events

- Ministry circulars and regulator's circulars

- Google alerts about the industry

- International news about the industry in other countries

One of the important aspects here is to correctly understand and comprehend the competitor's interviews and interpretations. Here, an important model suggested by Michael Porter—Competitor Analysis—is used. All communication by the management is broken down into parts and different segments are identified in different baskets—assumptions, strategy, capabilities and goals. Parts of interviews are identified, which helps one understand the competitors' goals, the strategy selected to get there, competitors' capabilities, which include strength and weaknesses, and lastly, the underlying assumptions of the management. Once understanding of different players is achieved, the firm can decide on the goals that they wish to achieve and the strategies they wish to follow. This is one of the critical exercises on being updated about the industry and its participants.

Third Tier

In the first tier, a macro scenario of the industry, the players involved, and the value chain were established. The second tier of the broad industry analysis focussed on more objective topics such as market size, pricing power, and government regulations. With this, an understanding of the structure of the industry being analysed was achieved. In the third tier, an attempt is made to determine the industry profitability based on the influence of the industry. This tier is built around the concept of Five Competitive Forces for Industry Analysis suggested by Michael Porter. This tier focusses on the ability of an industry to retain its profitability based on the competitive forces acting on it.

Porter's Five Forces

Porter's Five Forces is a model that identifies and analyses the five competitive forces that shape every industry, which help determine an industry's weaknesses and strengths. It is a business analysis model that helps explain why different industries are able to sustain different levels of profitability.[25] The model's biggest strength is that it can be applied to any segment of the economy. The model was first published in

---

[25] https://www.investopedia.com/terms/p/porter.asp

Michael E. Porter's book *Competitive Strategy: Techniques for Analysing Industries and Competitors*, in 1980. Porter identifies the five forces that act on each industry and are used to measure competitive intensity, attractiveness and profitability. An unattractive industry is one in which the effect of these five forces reduce the overall profitability.[26]

These five factors are:

— Supplier power

— Buyer power

— Threat of substitution

— Threat of entry

— Competitive intensity within the industry

Instead of developing a subjective opinion on the influence of each force on the industry, the industry must make an effort to bring objectivity in the process. This is done by breaking down each force into a series of questions and trying to evaluate the impact through each of these questions. These questions relate to the factors that determine the overall influence of each force on the profitability of the industry.

• **Supplier Power**

Supplier power refers to the bargaining power that suppliers of different raw materials have with the industry. It is their ability to drive up the prices of the raw materials required to make the products. Suppliers who have a very high bargaining power can, with ease, increase the price of the raw materials for the industry, and thus reduce the profitability of the industry, shifting it towards themselves.

---

[26]   https://thejournal.ng/2020/01/15/porters-5-forces-jim-chappelow/

The industry must check the supplier power of the supplier group for each factor of production. The power of supplier groups of each raw material must be checked. For analytical purposes, labour groups are also seen as suppliers of effort. Thus, this analytical framework should be applied for supplier power of labour and staff as well. All major inputs must be checked for their ability to increase prices with ease. Any single group of supplier that may refuse to work with the industry or charge excessively high prices can significantly reduce the industry's profitability.

Supplier power in an industry can be judged by a number of factors. These factors together decide the supplier power in the industry.

#Number of Suppliers in the Market

(Monopoly/Duopoly/Few/Many/Excess Supply)

Greater the number of suppliers for a product, lesser is the supplier power that the industry will face. This is because more firms are willing to sell the same product, allowing the buyer the option to choose from a competitive market. Thus, no supplier is able to dictate terms. In monopoly, there is a single source of supply, and the supplier can dictate terms about the supply of the product. In duopoly and oligopoly, it is the competitive relation and coordination between the firms that determines profitability. If the firms are well-coordinated and do not indulge in price competition, the suppliers as a group will have a high bargaining power. When there are many suppliers or excess supply, it generally turns out to be a buyers' market with a lower bargaining power for suppliers.

Thus, the number of suppliers is an important factor to judge supplier power. For labour and staff, supplier power can be judged by how well organised the labour groups are. Organised labour unions increase the bargaining power for them.

#Availability of Regular Supply

(Easy/Moderate/Difficult/Seasonal or Non-Seasonal)

Not all raw materials are available all the time with ease. The degree of irregularity in supplies requires firms to plan in advance and maintain buffer stocks of raw materials, so as to avoid losing production time. Also, at times there can be long dry spells of supply. When supply comes back, suppliers can find themselves with a high supplier power and increase prices. Thus, regular availability of supply reduces the bargaining power of suppliers. If availability is easy, firms in the industry will always have a choice and thus face low supplier power. On the other hand, difficulty in regular supply can give power to suppliers who have supplies available at that moment. Also, supply can be seasonal. If it is so, the product has to be stored. Due to spike in demand, suppliers can have a significant bargaining power during periods of supply.

#Uniqueness of Services (Availability of Substitutes for Raw Materials)

(Close substitutes/Distant substitutes/No substitutes)

Raw materials that have no substitutes and are unique (such as speciality chemicals with particular specifications that have no substitutes in producing pharmaceutical drugs) are not affected by the prices of any supplementary product industry, thus providing the suppliers a high bargaining power. If the services and supplies by the supplier group are unique, the supplier group will have high bargaining power. However, if close substitutes are available, the industry will have a choice and suppliers cannot increase prices at will and hurt industry profitability. In case of distant substitutes, industry participants will switch only if the difference is too large. This gives some degree of supplier power to make small increases in the prices but they still cannot increase prices at will and hurt industry profitability.

In case of labour, the uniqueness of skills required for the job and substitute of that skill-set determines the degree of bargaining power that they will possess.

#Ability to Substitute (Cost/Technology/Time/Effort)

(Easy/Moderate/Difficult/Cannot switch)

One thing is to have substitutes available, another is the ability to actually substitute. It takes cost, time, effort and technological reorientation to substitute a raw material with another one. If the ability is low and it is difficult to substitute, despite availability, the suppliers see it as an opportunity. Thus, they can gain by increasing prices due to the supplier power that they have. At the same time, if the industry can easily switch between raw materials, the suppliers have no bargaining power and are not able to increase industry profitability. Thus, the ease in substituting is a key factor in determining the bargaining power of suppliers.

#Switching Cost (Cost/Technology/Time/Effort/ Production Loss)

Despite having the ability to switch between substitutes, the switch does include some costs. These costs can be in multiple forms. There can be financial costs involved in switching or may require technology change in capital goods or retraining of labour. The entire process of switch may take a long period of time or the effort required might be too high. There may be a production loss. Switching costs can also be psychological in nature or, in many cases, the market may not accept the output produced. Thus, there is a large array of potential costs attached to the switch. Larger the cost, larger should be the benefit derived from the switch, so that the industry actually makes the switch. Thus, when the switching costs are high, the industry does not switch to substitutes easily. This gives the suppliers a bargaining power over the industry. Low switching costs allow the industry to negotiate with suppliers and thus benefit from it.

#Dependency of Industry on Them (Suppliers Need the Industry Less Than Industry Needs Them)

(High/Moderate/Low)

Some industries are highly dependent on a particular supplier industry for their survival. At the same time, other supplier industries are less critical for the success of the given industry. Here, the performance of the supplier's product determines the industry's end product performance. The industry can be said to be dependent on the supplier group, and the suppliers will have a very high bargaining power.

Another factor that influences dependence is the number of substitutes. If there are no substitutes for the product, the industry is dependent on the suppliers, thus giving them supplier power. On the flip side, some suppliers are dependent on the given industry. This is because the products they produce are only consumed in that given industry and no other industry uses the product. If multiple industries are using the product, the suppliers would be less dependent on the given industry. Thus, the industry that depends more on the other one will have less bargaining power.

#Can the Industry Threaten to Vertical`ly Integrate into its Suppliers Business?

(Yes/No)

Based on the entry barriers of the business of the supplier, if the industry poses a threat to suppliers to vertically integrate into their business, the firms in the industry will always have a bargaining power over the suppliers. The suppliers would always be under threat of new entry as their customer industry would emerge as their competitors.

Also, benefits of synergies derived for the industry from vertical integration would put the supplier firms in a position of competitive disadvantage.

#Importance of Volume to Suppliers

(High/Moderate/Low)

The businesses that have a high degree of operating leverage, i.e. high percentage of fixed costs against total costs, require volume in business, so as to cover the fixed costs. Also, other businesses that have low profit margins focus on the asset turnover for return on capital. Such businesses also need volume. If the supplier's business happens to be one such business, where the importance of volume is very high, suppliers would focus on increasing the volume for their sales rather than the prices. In such cases, where the supplier cannot afford to lose volume, they do not increase the prices too aggressively. Thus, the importance of volume for the supplier for its success limits the bargaining power and reduces the influence of supplier power over the industry.

#Payment Power With Buyer (Trade Credit Given)

One of the clear indicators of supplier power over an industry is the structure of credit given to the buyers. Generally, the suppliers with a greater bargaining power will have payment terms in their favour. If trade credits are given for very long periods of time, suppliers will have to put in more capital, stretching the working capital investments. This will limit the growth of suppliers, as, for every incremental growth, they will have to put in more capital into the business. Since capital is always limited, growth will also be limited. At the same time, if short credits are given, the buyer industry will have to put in more working capital and this will limit their growth. Thus, the supplier with a higher bargaining power is able to adjust the trade credit terms, so as to benefit from the same—by reducing the capital requirements.

A shorter credit duration means a high supplier power, whereas long and undisciplined credit duration means lower supplier power. However, credit terms can be seen as a test for bargaining power only between the immediate buyers and sellers. If an intermediary is involved, the credit terms will explain the balance of power between the supplier and the intermediary and not the supplier and the actual buyer.

The factors discussed earlier can be examined for an industry and together they can help evaluate the supplier power over the industry and the impact that suppliers have on the industry's profitability. A high supplier power makes the industry less attractive. Understanding the supplier power is critical for both the entrepreneur as well as the investor.

• Buyer Power

Buyer power refers to the bargaining power that different segments of buyers have over the industry. It is the ability of the customer to put the firm under pressure to keep the final price of the product low. This affects the customer's sensitivity towards price changes. Firms try to bring down the customer's bargaining power so that they can drive up the prices and increase profitability. For the purpose of analysis, if middlemen or distribution channels are involved, the buyer power of these middlemen as well as the end buyer is checked as both have the power to pressurise firms to reduce prices.

Buyers have a high bargaining power if firms find it difficult to increase the prices in the industry. Like supplier power, buyer power too can be judged by a number of factors. These will together decide the buyer power over the industry.

#Number of Buyers/Customers

(Single/Few/Many/Mass)

The concentration of buyers significantly influences the bargaining power that buyers have over the given industry. If there is only one or a few buyers for the industry's products, each buyer would buy in large volumes. Thus, the buyer(s) would be able to dictate the terms and benefit from the bargaining power. At the same time, a large number of buyers or a mass market for the product means no single buyer can dictate terms. Thus, buyers won't have a significant bargaining power. However, in case the buyers are able to organise themselves and a large number of buyers can come together, they can collectively negotiate with the industry and gain bargaining power.

#Size of Buyers/Orders

(Several small orders/A few medium-sized/Single very large order)

The size and frequency of order by buyers is an important factor influencing the buyer's bargaining power. If there are several small orders placed by the buyers, the industry's dependence on any single order decreases, thus decreasing the buyer's bargaining power. However, if a few medium-sized orders or a single very large order can be placed, each order becomes critical for the industry and the industry players cannot lose orders in negotiations. This reduces the industry's bargaining power and the buyers are successfully able to pressurise the industry to reduce prices, thus impacting industry profitability.

#How Informed Are the Buyers?

(Very informed/Moderately informed/Uninformed/Ignorant)

In this age of information, any information regarding any purchase decision that needs to be made is very readily informed by the industry.

Most buyers today do their research before they go out to make a purchase. In the process, they figure out all the various options that they have—prices of the products, value propositions they are offered, etc. As buyers are more informed, they select the option that is the best fit for their needs at the lowest price. Thus, informed buyers force the industry to be competitive in terms of prices. This reduces industry profitability.

In industries where the buyers are not very well-informed, firms are able to increase the prices, as the buyer is not aware of possible cheaper choices. Also, in many cases, the purchase may not be very critical as it could be a one-time buy or the price is a very small percentage of the total income of the buyers. In such cases, the buyer makes no attempt to get proper information and is ignorant of the choices that he may have. So, informed buyers, due to their purchase behaviour, pressurise the industry to reduce prices. So, more informed the buyers are, higher would be their bargaining power.

#Price Sensitivity of Buyers

(Perfectly inelastic/Inelastic/Elastic/Perfectly elastic)

The degree of elasticity of demand refers to the degree to which demand changes against changes in the price of the product. If the change is high, the demand is said to be elastic and vice versa. If the buyer's price sensitivity is elastic, it limits the ability of the industry to increase prices. At times, the buyers may even have to reduce prices to increase demand. At the same time, an inelastic demand allows the industry to increase prices, as increase in prices does not reduce the demand. Thus, elastic demand gives buyers a higher bargaining power, as they can reduce consumption and therefore pressurise the industry to reduce prices.

#Demand-Supply Scenario

(Excess demand, balance, excess supply)

The demand-supply scenario allows the industry to determine prices and, thus, profitability. Since the situation that would exist would be known to both—the industry firms and the buyers, they can use it as a point of determining bargaining power between them. In industries where there is excess demand, the sellers are the selectors and they can determine the prices that show a reduced buyer power. At the same time, in industries where there is excess supply, the buyers are the selectors and they gain buyer power. In a balanced state, no one gets a significant bargaining power.

#Can the Buyers Threaten to Vertically Integrate into Business?

(Yes/No)

Backward integration brings with it various cost-related advantages as well as more control over the supply chain. These benefits can be significant to any firm. However, backward integration often comes at a cost against these benefits. There could also be significant entry barriers into the industry. Based on the cost-benefit analysis and the entry barriers, it may or may not be viable for an industry's customers to backward integrate. If the industry's buyers can backward integrate and replace the supplier firm, they stand to gain a significant bargaining power over the industry. The buyers can constantly pressurise the suppliers to not increase prices or else they may themselves backward integrate. The ability to backward integrate increases the buyer's power over the industry.

#Payment Power With Buyers

(Terms of credit given)

As with supplier power, buyer power can also be judged by the terms of credit given. If the buyers can negotiate for a longer credit duration, the excess working capital would be put in by the industry's firms. This would limit growth as every incremental growth would require an additional capital input from the industry. However, if the industry allows only a short credit period, the buyers would have to put in the additional working capital and this would limit their growth. The one who can negotiate favourable credit terms is said to have a higher bargaining power. Longer the credit given, higher is the buyer power over the industry.

The factors discussed collectively influence the buyer's bargaining power over the industry. Significant buyer power limits profitability for the industry and makes it less attractive.

•   Threat of Substitution

A substitute product uses a different technology to try and solve the same economic need.[27] This refers to the attempt to create similar gains or relieving same pains, even though different technology is used. Industries that have close substitutes are always under threat of being replaced by other products. The customers will always be weighing the value propositions of the substitute products and their prices. The moment the value proposition of other products becomes stronger than the product they are currently using, they may start switching over.

At the same time, industries that have no close substitute allow their firms more power to increase prices and lock in more favourable terms. There are a number of factors that together influence the threat of substitution for an industry.

---

[27]   https://yourfreetemplates.com/porters-five-forces-template/

#Availability of Substitute for the Goods

(Close substitute/Distant substitute/No substitute)

The first and most important factor while determining the threat of substitution for an industry is availability of substitutes. If there are no substitutes available, there ends the matter, with no current threat of substitution. However, if substitutes are available, they can be close or distant ones. Close substitutes are those that very closely meet the exact needs of the customers whereas distant substitutes are not exact replacements for the product but they can be used with a few modifications. For instance, corn flakes and oats are close substitutes for each other whereas a mobile phone and a tablet are distant substitutes.

The threat of substitutes is highest when close substitutes are available. As the value propositions are compared, if the substitute offers even a slightly better value for the price paid, the customer will switch over. At the same time, though distant substitutes are potential threats, the buyer will switch only if the difference in the value proposition is significantly high. This gives more flexibility to the industry to price their products. Closer the substitute is, the more motivated the buyer is to switch. Thus, higher would be the threat of substitution for the industry.

#Ability to Substitute

(Easy/Moderate/Difficult/No substitutes)

Despite availability of substitutes, actual substitution takes time, cost, effort and technological reorientation. Some substitutions are very easy to make, whereas others can be challenging. If the ability of the buyers to make the switch is very high i.e. it is easy for them to do so, the threat of substitution would be very high, which would reduce industry profitability. If it is difficult to switch, even with the availability of substitutes, the threat of substitution for the industry would weaken and allow firms flexibility in pricing their products.

#Cost of Substitution

(Cost/Technology/Habit/Time/Effort)

Even if substitutes for an industry are readily available and the ability to substitute is also high, the actual substitution still involves a number of costs, which act as impediments to substitution. They can be in the form of financial cost, technological reorientation, time, effort, and psychological cost. If the costs of substitution are relatively high, the buyer's willingness to substitute might reduce. Thus, a higher cost of substitution allows the industry pricing flexibility and reduces the threat of substitution. A higher cost of substitution makes the industry more attractive by increasing profitability.

#Price Performance of Substitute Compared to Industry's Product

(Better price/Better performance/Unfavourable)

All purchase decisions are based on comparing the price against the performance of the different products available. The price performance determines the value proposition strength of the product; the product with the stronger proposition gets accepted. This involves comparing the price and performance of the substitute against the industry's product. The point is to figure out if the substitute is cheaper than the industry's product with a matching performance or if it performs better at the same price. The greater the difference, the higher will be the threat of substitution. However, there may be many scenarios where the current price performance of the substitute is unfavourable. This would mean a relatively lower threat of substitution currently, but it can affect the industry going forward. Thus, the strength in the value proposition of the substitute against the industry's product and the magnitude of difference determine the threat of substitution. Evaluating this factor involves subjectivity to a certain extent.

The factors discussed together decide if the industry needs to compete with any other industry due to threat of substitution. Higher the threat, lower would be the industry's profitability.

• Threat of Entry

Profitable industries that yield high returns are attractive to new entrants. New entrants will decrease the profitability for other firms in the industry unless the entry can be made difficult for these new firms by creating entry barriers.[28] The less time and money it takes for a competitor to enter a company's market and be an effective competitor, the more vulnerable the industry would be to the threat of new entrants. An industry with strong barriers to entry allows the firms in the industry to charge high prices and thus gain bargaining power. A number of factors together decide the threat of new entrants to an industry.

#Time and Cost of Sizeable Entry

(Very High/High/Moderate/Low)

Entry into any industry and then gaining size to become a significant entrant that can challenge the established firms requires time and capital investment. The costs associated with such an entry forms a part of the entry barriers. Higher the time and cost of sizeable entry into any industry, lower would be the threat from entrants that the industry's existing firms will face. However, newer business models and value propositions, backed by venture capitalists and private equity

---

[28]   https://en.wikipedia.org/wiki/Substitute_product

firms, have often been able to overcome an otherwise expensive entry barrier. No business and industry can feel secure against the threat of new entrants as disruptive forces are acting on all industries in some form or the other.

#Economies of Scale

(High/Moderate/Low)

One of the important entry barriers in a business is the presence of economies of scale. This provides early-mover advantage to the incumbents and makes it difficult for challengers to enter and gain scale. Higher the economies of scale in an industry, higher will be relative competitive advantage of the incumbents. As these firms are at a position of advantage, newer demand will also move towards them. At the same time, challengers will have to gain same volume to stand at an equal footing else their offering would be incompetent. As volume advantage to incumbent keeps getting bigger and bigger, new entrants find it very difficult to successfully enter the industry. So, it is seen that higher the economies of scale, higher would be the advantage to incumbents and lower would be the threat to entry.

#Distribution Strength Required

(High/Moderate/Low)

Some industries are designed in such a manner that they need distribution strength for success. Building distribution strength requires time, effort and cost and these can be entry barriers. If the distribution strength required in an industry is high and it is critical for success in the industry, the threat of entry would be low as any new entrant will need time to build distribution. It will also be more expensive for an entrant to build distribution channels as they will have to offer higher margins to the middlemen. However, industries should be wary about new technologies and business models that can reduce the need for traditional distribution strength.

#Cost Advantages to Existing Players (Location/Unique Resources)

(Yes/No)

Location or access to unique resources can be a great source of competitive advantage to the existing players in any industry. Location can reduce logistics cost for players if they are strategically located near the raw materials or the markets. Also, there might be low availability of space in the surroundings for new entrants to set shop, thus forcing them to a location that is relatively less attractive. Such cost advantages for existing players can make access to the industry difficult, thus reducing threat of entrants.

Also, unique resources with a firm cannot be accessed by any other entrant. Cost benefits from these resources cannot be copied by entrants, thus making entry into the industry difficult.

#Switching Costs for Customers Within the Industry

(Cost/Technology/Hassle/Habit/Knowledge/Dependency/None)

Switching between the players of the same industry that have similar offerings also involves costs. These include financial costs, technological reorientation, psychological costs like hassle and habit, knowledge and database with the previous company, and process dependency with previous company. Switching at times require a lot of effort. Many times, it might even be a very complex goal to achieve. Presence of switching costs makes it difficult for entrants to enter an industry and make buyers switch from other player's products. This allows established players greater pricing power over their products – by reducing the threat of new entrants.

#Asset Specificity in Industry

(Geographical specificity/dedicated assets are assets for a specific buyer or transaction. Human specificity is specific technical knowledge of labour.)

Some industries have assets that are specific to them and these cannot be put to any alternative use. Such industries have high exit costs in situations of failure of the firm. The high exit costs and risky capital expenditure upfront discourage new investments within the industry. For instance, some assets that have been used in a particular geography cannot be shifted or moved to another use. They can be used only for that particular purpose. For example, modern warehouse structures and metro projects. If the business becomes unviable in a particular geography, not much can be done to shift the assets or put them to a different use.

There are also dedicated assets, which are built specifically for the needs of the buyers or for particular orders, and they cannot be put to any other use. There can be specificity in the knowledge and skills of labour too. Once the labour is trained for a particular industry, it may be very difficult for them to work in any other industry. Such specificity in assets makes investments risky and discourages entry. Thus, high asset specificity in the industry reduces the threat of entry in the industry.

#Proprietary Product Difference

(High/Medium/Low)

Two generic strategies can be pursued – being the lowest cost producer in the industry or being a strategy of differentiation. In industries where firms have successfully differentiated their products, entry becomes difficult for new players as there is no generic product to compete with initially. If the sources of differentiation are proprietary, the entrants cannot even make low-cost variants of the existing product. Thus, if proprietary product differentiation in an industry is high, entrants are unable to match the products of existing players. Thus, the threat of substitution is reduced. This allows the existing players flexibility in pricing their products.

#Network Effect of the Product

(Yes/No)

The key question to ask when identifying network effect is: how does a customer benefit if more consumers use the product? Network effect occurs when a group of consumers meet over a platform and together solve their needs through sharing of information or products. As a small network is established on a platform, more and more consumers are attracted towards it; over time it gains in size, and the network effect becomes stronger and stronger. Each new user has no choice but to opt for that particular network. Network effect gives a huge first-mover advantage and the challengers find it very difficult to enter – as the network tends to be very sticky and does not move unless the difference in the offering is huge. Thus, presence of network effect reduces the threat of new entrants.

#Protection Against New Entrants

(Patents/Licences/Technology intellectual property/Trademarks/ Proprietary intangible assets)

Established firms are protected against new entrants due to the legal protection they have earned on the assets they have created over time. For instance, firms may have earned patents on their research and development results; they may have special licenses, trademarks or proprietary intangibles, which cannot be imitated by other firms in the industry. If this protection is on assets that are critical for success in the industry, new entrants would not be able to access them. This reduces the threat from new entrants. It allows the established firms flexibility to price their products and increase profitability.

#Brand Identity

(High/Moderate/Low)

One of the important intangibles that protects industries against new firms is the power of the established brands of incumbents. If 'brands' is one of the key factors based on which the purchase decision is made in the industry, it becomes very difficult for new entrants to find success – as brands cannot be established overnight and brands of established firms are far more recognised than others. Therefore, the switch from old firms to new entrants becomes very difficult. It can be said that higher the importance of brands while making the purchase decision and more powerful the brands of established firms are, the lower would be the threat of new entrants. Pricing power with the established firms would not allow new entrants to reduce profitability. However, if brands are not very critical while making the purchase decision, even existence of strong brands cannot stop the low-end entrants to the industry.

#Reputation of Existing Firms

(Important for success/Not important for success)

Some businesses are businesses of reputation or goodwill, as reputation is required for success in the industry. For instance, in most financial institutions, business is achieved only if the firm has a good reputation. In such businesses, entrants cannot build reputation overnight and this acts as a big competitive disadvantage for them, making entry itself difficult. Thus, in businesses where reputation is very critical for getting more business, entry is difficult and thus the threat of entry is reduced.

#Expected Reaction by Established Firms to New Entrants

(Panic/Moderate strategic response/No reaction)

Every entrant to an industry is met with retaliation of different degrees, based on the outcome or impact that the entrant is expected to have.

Some large entrants are feared by the established players and the entry of such entrants creates panic in the industry. The established players retaliate with aggressive measures such as price wars, advertisement wars, and product launches and they mostly end up hurting the industry profitability.

Other firms receive a moderate response that is strategic in nature and takes time. Such a response aims to deal with entrants strategically, making it difficult for them to gain size by putting them at a position of competitive disadvantage. Such industries, more often than not, do not hurt the industry profitability. However, the risk remains that, if the strategic response goes wrong, firms may lose market to the entrant.

Many entrants may receive no reaction at all from established firms. Established firms do not see the entrants as threats and decide to not react to them. Such a strategy does not hurt profitability in the short run, but it has the risk of the entrant taking away market from the established players. Thus, the expected retaliation to entry by existing players is an important factor that decides the impact on profitability. More aggressive the response is, greater is the impact on profitability and higher is the threat of new entrants.

The above-said factors determine the ability of new entrants to enter the industry and the response of existing firms, which determines the impact of entry on profitability. These together determine the threat of entry to existing firms. Higher the threat, lower would be the profitability of the industry.

- **Competitive Rivalry**

For most industries, the intensity of competitive rivalry is one of the major determinants of industry profitability. In some industries, the players have a cutthroat battle whereas in others, the players learn to live with peace. Each of them finds a place in the market for themselves and do not eye each other's market share too aggressively.

This force refers to the number of competitors and their ability and willingness to undercut each other. Higher the ability and willingness, more will the companies undercut each other, thus reducing the overall industry profitability. Suppliers and buyers look to interact with industries with a high competitive intensity as they can seek out competition if they are unable to offer a better deal or lower prices. Conversely, when competitive rivalry is low, a company has greater power to charge higher prices and set the terms of deals.[29]

Like other forces, competitive rivalry and its intensity is influenced by multiple factors. All the factors together help evaluate the competitive rivalry between industry participants. These have been discussed going forward.

#Number of Major Competitors in the Industry

(1, 2, 3..., A few, Many)

The competitive intensity of an industry depends upon the ability of competitors to communicate with each other and work in a harmonious manner, wherein the actions of no firm hurt the overall industry profitability. The ability to communicate depends on the number of competitors in the industry. Higher the number of competitors, more difficult will it be for the competitors to communicate effectively and

---

[29]   https://www.investopedia.com/terms/p/porter.asp

work in harmony. Also, a large number of firms means a large number of different strategies being used, each having the potential to hurt industry profitability. As a result, higher the number of competitors in the industry, greater would be the competitive intensity and lower would be the general industry profitability.

#How Concentrated is the Industry?

(Concentrated/Moderately diluted/Very dilute)

Another factor, in line with the number of competitors in the industry, which influences the rivalry, is the concentration of the industry. The way market share is distributed among the competitors has a major impact on their ability to dictate terms and impact competitive rivalry. If a single firm has a majority market share or a few large firms have the majority market and they do not indulge in intense rivalry, the remaining firms are merely followers and they are not able to intensify the competition a lot. At the same time, industries that are moderately diluted or very diluted in terms of distribution of market share find it very difficult to communicate effectively. Due to the absence of a clear market leader, all firms have the ability to impact the intensity of competition by initiating price cuts. Thus, more concentrated the industry, lower would be the probability of firms that get involved in intense competition. This will allow the industry to retain profitability and increase attractiveness.

#Differences in Product Quality

(Homogenous/Minor differences/Major differences)

An important factor that impacts the challenger's ability to undercut prices and sell their products is the difference between the quality of products of the various competitors. If the products are homogenous or have minor differences, the purchase decision depends on the price alone. Here, the firms can successfully undercut each other to gain market share. However, if the differences are major, the purchase decisions are not solely based on prices. Here, the firms cannot undercut each other to gain market share. Those with superior quality would still attract business.

However, the challenge here is: will the quality be perceived by the buyers? Even if there are major differences in quality, if they are not understood by the buyers, the purchase decision would still be based on price alone. Then the competitors will gain the power to undercut each other. So, differences in product quality is a major factor in determining competitive intensity, provided they are communicated to the buyers clearly.

#Cost of Switching

(Brand/Cost/Technology/Hassle/Habit/Knowledge/Dependency/None)

Switching to competitor products requires time and effort. It has a cost associated with it. The switch should give the buyers a net advantage even after bearing the switching costs. Switching costs include financial costs, effort, technological reorientation, and psychological factors such as hassle, change in habit, and affinity towards brand. The buyers' systems and processes may depend on the firm's products and making a switch would require redesigning of processes. Thus, switching costs at times reduce the buyer's ability to switch; at other times they demotivate the buyer from switching to another product. Only if the benefit is substantial will the customer be willing to switch. This cannot be achieved by merely undercutting competition. Thus, higher the switching costs, lower would be the competitive intensity within the industry.

#Is the Industry Growing?

(Fast growth/Moderate growth/Zero growth/Negative growth)

All firms wish to grow; each leg of growth can come from different sources – industry growth, market share gain or entering a new industry altogether. No single firm has control over the pace of industry growth. Strategically speaking, firms can rely only on aggression for market share gain or choose to enter new industries. The pace of the industry growth is critical in determining the intensity of competition. If the industry is growing fast, all competitors can grow by gaining more from the new business. However, if the industry is growing slowly, the major source of gain is market share growth. Thus, in slow-growth industries, the competitors tend to compete very intensely with each other, as each of them wishes to benefit from the other firm's market share. So, faster the industry grows, lower would be the intensity of competition.

#Overcapacity in the Industry (Permanent or Seasonal)

(High/Medium/Low)

Industries can have permanent as well as seasonal excess installed capacity and underutilisation. Seasonal factors do not affect the competitive intensity as much as permanent overcapacity. Structural and long-term industry overcapacity incentivises competitors to be more aggressive. They try to gain market share so as to improve the production in volume terms. High overcapacity would lead to intense competition in the industry whereas reducing overcapacity would lead to less intense competition. Overdemand causes firms to not undercut each other and thus achieve higher profitability.

#Fixed Costs in the Industry

(High/Medium/Low)

Some industries structurally have a higher proportion of fixed costs in their cost structure. Such companies wish to produce as much volume of products as possible in order to distribute the fixed costs over a larger volume of products and reduce the per-unit fixed costs of production. So, in order to gain market and volume, these companies may be willing to produce for a lower realisation of the product. As a result, the competitors undercut each other to gain volume. So it can be concluded that industries with a higher proportion of fixed costs than variable costs are incentivised to compete aggressively and face intense competition within the industry. This reduces the overall profitability of the industry.

#Exit Barriers in the Industry

(High/Medium/Low)

As per the laws of economics, firms tend to operate till the time they are able to cover their fixed costs. Below this, they reach their shutdown point and it is not advisable for them to continue operating. However, some industries have exit barriers associated with them. For instance, the inability to collect account receivables in time if they shut down or the inability to sell physical assets. In such instances, firms continue to sell, despite reaching their shutdown level, and excess capacity tends to stay with the industry. This excess capacity does not allow the supply-demand situation to turn more favourable, and firms are forced to compete in an oversupplied market. This causes them to indulge in undercutting each other. Thus, high industry barriers in industry reduce overall profitability by intensifying competitive rivalry.

#Basis of Competition in the Industry

(Price advertising/Advertising/New products/Customer service)

Not all competition reduces profitability. Some forms of competition can benefit the industry as well. Competitors within an industry compete on various grounds—price, effectiveness of advertising, new products launched, and customer service provided.

Competition on the basis of price leads to firms undercutting each other and this impacts the profitability of the industry. Competition with respect to advertising adds to the firm's costs; but they may also increase the awareness about the industry and allow firms to price their products better. Such competition can be beneficial for the overall industry as well.

Competition through launch of products has costs associated with it, but it helps expand the scope of the industry and allows firms to grow faster due to new innovative products with more features and uses. Enhanced customer service also adds to the cost but it increases customer satisfaction, thus increasing the customer's willingness to pay.

The basis of competition decides whether the intensity of competition will benefit or hurt the industry. A favourable basis of competition can be a boom for the industry.

The factors discussed together decide the intensity of competitive rivalry within an industry. Intensity of competition, along with the basis of competition, decides the impact that competition will have on the overall industry profitability. Remember, not all competition is bad for the industry.

Together, all five forces (supplier power, buyer power, threat of substitution, threat of entry, and competitive intensity within the industry) determine the industry's profitability. However, when one looks at firm-wise performance, firm-specific factors also affect profitability. The profitability for average firms in a good industry might be at par with good firms in an average industry. So, the role of the analyst or the entrepreneur is to find out industries where the average profitability is high.

Another important aspect is to keep track of how the five forces change over time. Industry profitability keeps changing as firms deploy different strategies and industries evolve over time. Thus, the third tier deals with the understanding of current and potential industry profitability and the changing trends in the industry.

Supplier Power

Cost of substitution	No substitutes
Number of suppliers	Many
Availability of regular supply	Easy
Availability of substitutes	No substitutes
Dependency of the industry on suppliers	Moderate
Do suppliers threaten vertical integration	No
Importance of volume to suppliers	Low
Payment power with suppliers	Cash payment

Buyer Power

Number of buyers	Many
Size of buyers	A few medium-sized
How informed are the buyers	Very informed
Price sensitivity	Inelastic
Demand-supply scenario	Excess demand in organised segement
Do buyers threaten vertical integration	Yes
Payment power with buyers	Credit given (15-30 days)

Threat of Entrants

Time and cost of sizeable entry	Moderate
Economies of scale	High
Distribution strength required	High
Location / Unique resources with existing companies	No
Switching costs for customers	Hassle, technology, dependence
Asset specificity in the industry	High geographic specificity
Proprietory product difference	Low
Network effect advantages	Yes
IP protection against entrants	No protection
Reputation of existing companies	Reputation important to get orders
Expected response to entry by existing companies	Moderate strategic response

Threat of Substitutes

Availability of substitute	No
Ability to substitute	No
Cost of substituting	No
Price performance of substitute against industry's product	None

Competitive Rivalry within Industry

Number of major competitors	A few larger ones and many small ones
How concentrated or diluted is the industry	Moderately dilute
Differences in product quality	Minor
Cost of switching players	Dependency and hassle
Growth in the indsutry	Fast growth
Overcapacity in the industry	Seasonal
Fixed costs in the industry	High
Exit barriers in the industry	Moderate exit barriers
Basis of competition in the industry	Price and service competition

Conclusion
- Moderate buyer power as smaller players have no power but larger ones like Amazon and Flipkart have significant power
- Low supplier power. Staff, fleet owners and warehouse owners are the suppliers. Till the time they are not organised, they have low bargaining power
- No threat of substitution
- Firms can start and gain scale in pockets of market but gaining pan-India entry is difficult. Moderate risk as threat of entry through acquisition exists
- Moderate competition as homogeneous product in a fast-growing industry competing on price and service
- Logistics should enjoy average profitability due to above-said impact of the five forces

Fourth Tier

The first three tiers of the broad industry analysis deal with the qualitative characteristics of an industry. The focus is on the way the industry operates, its value chain, the value map generated, and then the market size, industry stability, pricing power, and government regulations. This is followed by an understanding of the industry attractiveness based on Porter's five forces. The tiers give us a qualitative understanding of how the industry is placed and the forces that affect its attractiveness and profitability.

The last tier of the broad industry analysis deals with the quantitative analysis of the attractiveness of the industry. It compares return metrics, cash flow and investment requirements of players in the industry. The qualitative factors of the industry can be validated through the quantitative performance of firms in the industry.

In this tier, certain firms have to be selected from the industry. They should be chosen based on market share or through randomness i.e. using no filter at all. The number of firms selected can vary based on their concentration in the market. More concentrated the industry is, higher the number of firms that should be chosen. As a rule of thumb, four players give a good enough understanding of the whole industry. They cover a relatively wide range of strategies, firm-specific factors and management factors so that one particular factor does not affect the result of our entire analysis. However, this is true only if firms are chosen with complete randomness and no biases. Given that there is still a possibility that firm-specific factors of these players can affect our analysis, it can be reduced further by increasing the number of firms in the sample. On the whole, the analysis gives a good picture of the current quantitative performance of the industry. The common metrics are evaluated so as to understand the quantitative performance of the industry. These include an analysis of the return on equity and return on capital and breaking them down for DuPont analysis. Further, investment needs and cash flow generating ability of the industry are evaluated.

The common metrics to evaluate quantitative performance of the industry are:

ROE and ROCE Analysis

Return on equity (ROE) refers to profit earned after taxes on each rupee invested as equity in the business. Equity refers to the amount invested by the owners in the business and the sum of earnings retained within the business over the years. ROE is the most important metric to evaluate the return earned by the owners of the business. Higher the return on equity, lower would be the equity investment required to produce a certain profit. High ROE businesses are valued very highly.

ROE can be broken down into three components to understand the source of return for the business.

ROE = PAT / Shareholder's equity

= PAT / Revenue × Revenue / Assets × Assets / Equity

= PAT margin × Asset turnover × Leverage

ROE can be generated through high profit margin, high asset turnover or leverage. The source of return is very critical for the business. Return in industries with high margin means the industry must be very attractive qualitatively or else the margin would not sustain. A high turnover business is generated when the assets are efficiently utilised and the business does not require excessive capital investment. A higher ROE can also be generated through greater leverage in the industry by stretching the balance sheet to buy assets using borrowed money i.e. debt. Though this increases the ROE, a higher leverage can be risky for the company. This is because, as it magnifies profits, it also magnifies losses and their impact.

The trend in ROE over time for various companies in the industry and the source of ROE determine the quantitative attractiveness of the industry.

Another metric that is used to determine quantitative performance is Return on capital employed (ROCE). It refers to the return earned on all capital invested in the business i.e. equity and debt. ROCE evaluates the overall operating returns from the business and not just from the owner.

ROCE = EBIT / Capital employed

= EBIT / Revenue × Revenue / Capital employed

= EBIT margin × Capital turnover

ROCE mainly comes from two sources – margins and turnover. ROCE is not affected by the financing decisions of the industry. This is the primary reason why ROCE uses earnings before interest and tax (EBIT) and not profit after tax.

ROCE is compared with weighted average cost of capital. A business that earns less than its cost of capital would destroy the value for its owners, whereas one that earns more than the cost of capital would create value for the owners.

WACC = Cost of equity × Weight of equity +
Cost of debt (1 - tax rate) × Weight of debt

Other important metric that shows the quantitative performance of the industry is the growth rate within the industry. Revenue growth rate and profit growth rate over time show the growth of various firms in the industry. They can indicate the overall behaviour of the industry over a period of time.

Growth rate must be compared to sustainable growth rate within the industry. Sustainable growth rate (SGR) is the rate of growth a company can sustain without any external capital, provided its ROE does not change. It is calculated as follows:

SGR = ROE (1 - Dividend payout ratio)

Dividend payout ratio is the percentage of total profits that is paid out as dividends. So, if a firm earns an ROE of 15% and pays out 33% of its earnings as dividend, its sustainable growth rate would be 15% (1 - 0.33) = 10%. A company can grow beyond its sustainable growth rate continuously, either through investment of new capital or by improving its ROE going forward. However, SGR analysis of the industry is affected by the dividend payout strategies of various firms. But it can give an overall understanding of growth in the industry and the need for external capital for such growth.

ROE and ROCE Analysis for Asian Paints Ltd - Indian Paint Industry

(All amounts are in Rs. crores)

	2016	2017	2018	2019
Equity	6525	7604	8410	9520
PAT	1745	1939	2039	2159
Return on equity	26.74%	25.50%	24.24%	22.68%
Revenue	14271	15062	16825	19342
Operating assets	4956	5412	5755	8356
Margin	12.22%	12.87%	12.11%	11.11%
Asset t/o	2.88	2.78	2.92	2.31
Leverage	0.76	0.72	0.68	0.87
EBIT	2725	2994	3204	3530
Return on assets	54.98%	55.32%	55.67%	42.24%
Dividend payout ratio	41%	51%	41%	47%
Sustainable growth rate	15.76%	12.38%	14.31%	12.02%
Revenue growth	4.9%	5.55%	11.71%	14.95%
PAT growth	25.09%	11.11%	5.16%	5.88%

Free Cash Flow Analysis

- So, we see that Asian Paints in Paint industry has a margin >10%, asset turnover >2 and leverage < 1. The company shows decent growth.
- Such analysis can be done for 3-4 more companies in the same industry to draw generalisations about the entire industry.

Some businesses are cash-seeking businesses. This means they are always in need of additional cash. Some others are cash-producing businesses; they produce more cash than they need. It is very difficult to scale cash-heavy businesses as every leg of growth requires incremental investments whereas cash-producing businesses are able to fund themselves due to their cash-producing ability.

Free cash flow is a measure used to evaluate the industry's cash requirements. It has two components—cash flow from operations and fixed capital investments. Cash flow from operations (CFO) is the cash a business generates from the normal course of business after working capital investments. CFO is generated by the business every year. Fixed capital investment (FCI) refers to the operating capital expenditure by the business, which shall provide benefits for a period longer than a year. The difference between CFO and FCI refers to free cash flow i.e. excess cash left after meeting the investment needs of the business. Free cash flow is excess cash that can be taken away from the business without affecting the operations.

Cash-producing industries and firms are able to generate ample free cash flows, whereas cash-seeking industries may even produce a negative cash flow. Some industries are structurally such that they seek regular cash inflow, whereas others do not require as much cash investment. Free cash flow as a percentage of revenue must be used to compare the cash-producing abilities of firms across industries, relative to their size. Higher the ratio, greater is the cash-producing ability.

However, one must pay attention to the following fact. The investment needs of businesses may not be linear in nature; they may be rather lumpy. That is why free cash flow should always be seen over a period of time and not for any particular year. Companies in the middle of significant expansion may have a temporarily negative free cash flow.

Free Cash Flows Generated by Asian Paints Ltd

(All amounts are in Rs. crores)

	2016	2017	2018	2019
CFO	2243	1527	2113	2214
Interest paid	49	37	41	56
Fixed capital investment	(817)	(684)	(1425)	(1150)
Free cash flow	1475	880	729	1120
Revenues	14271	15062	16825	19342
FCF / Revenues	10.33%	5.84%	4.33%	5.79%

- It is seen that the company converts 5-6% of its revenues as free cash flows. The company is also not too fixed capital investment intensive and is continuously able to create FCF.
- Generalisations about the industry can be drawn after similar analysis for 2-3 companies in the same industry.

Industry Investment Requirements

Different industries have different investment requirements. Some are working capital heavy whereas others require high fixed capital investments. Some other businesses require very low investments. Such businesses scale very quickly. Thus, an important metric for attractiveness of an industry is its investment requirements. Fixed capital investment and working capital investments together determine investment requirements of businesses in the industry. They must be calculated as a percentage of revenue. Lower the investment required against revenue, more attractive is the industry.

The fourth tier allows the analyst to draw conclusions about the general quantitative performance of the industry.

The four tiers together form the 'basic industry analysis', which is the third point in the '9 -point business circuit'. It gives an understanding of the overall processes in the industry and the profitability characteristics. This stage is one of the most critical stages when attempting to understand any particular business. This four-tiered structure is equally valid for those looking to invest in businesses as well as those looking to start their own business. Such an analysis can be of great help to even those who are already running businesses of any kind.

Investment Needs of Asian Paints Ltd

(All amounts are in Rs. crores)

	2016	2017	2018	2019
Fixed capital investment	817	684	1425	1150
Working capital investment	(197)	602	79	427
Total investments	620	1286	1504	1577
Revenues	14271	15062	16825	19342
Investments / Revenues	4.33%	8.53%	8.93%	8.15%

- It is seen that the company has been investing 8-9% of its revenues into fixed capital and working capital for the last 3 years. Most of the investments are towards fixed assets. We see that the company is not operating in an asset-intensive industry as only a fraction of revenue is re-invested each year.
- Generalisations about the industry can be drawn after similar analysis for 2-3 companies in the same industry.

Evolution of the Industry

The first point of the 9-point circuit deals with understanding the value proposition of the industry and its constituent players. The second point relates to business models. It is a business-specific factor. As said earlier, this would be covered in the second book in the series. The third point deals with the basic industry analysis, which gives a much deeper understanding of the qualitative attractiveness of the industry, its value chain, and the demand-supply scenario. It also explains pricing power in the industry, industry stability, and the government's attitude towards the industry. It ends with an evaluation of the quantitative returns of the existing players and their ability to produce and consume cash.

The point 'evolution of industry and businesses' deals with how the industry, its products and the various firms within it have evolved over the years to arrive at the current stage. This stage is linked to the fourth point in 9-point business circuit. It gives a perspective of the history of the industry and thus allows entrepreneurs and investors to reason the current state more rationally. It gives them an understanding of what has worked in the industry in the past and what has not.

Like in biology, understanding evolution is critical in business too—to understand its past, present and future. Evolution is the only explanation for diversity in businesses. It also explains the similarities and differences in approaches, strategies and business models within the industry. It throws light on the changes that happen to the needs of customers, how their pains and gain requirements were born, how they have changed over time, and what different offerings were created in due course.

Just like it is in biology, the evolution of an industry is also based on the concepts of 'natural selection', 'adaptation' and 'survival of the fittest'.

In biology, natural selection refers to the mechanism of evolution where genetic mutations that are beneficial to an individual's survival chances are passed on through reproduction. This results in a new generation of organisms that are more likely to survive to reproduce. This leads to further adaptation by the organisms, which means physical or behavioural characteristics may change, allowing them to survive the environment better. Survival of the fittest means all those who are fit and have adapted themselves successfully are the ones who go on to survive. Those who fail to adapt are unable to survive and reproduce, and thus they get extinct.[30]

Let us apply these concepts to understand businesses and industries. Firms undergo changes which, according to them, shall increase their chances of survival and help them stay relevant for a longer period of time. The firms that undergo adaptation and make relevant changes continuously are the ones that survive longer; and the weaker ones die. Any given industry goes through multiple rounds of disruption, which expand its life span before it ceases to exist. Either the need to survive goes away or a substitute industry replaces it.

---

[30]   https://www.nhm.ac.uk/discover/what-is-natural-selection.html

When a new business model comes along, every player in the industry tries different strategies and creates new product offerings. This is adaptation for survival.

Understanding evolution allows analysts and entrepreneurs to better understand what has worked and what has failed in the industry. It helps them reason better about why things are the way they are in the industry. It also prevents them from repeating the many mistakes that have already been made.

For new businesses that are being started, which shall establish a new industry going forward, the research should focus on understanding the evolution of the needs of the customer segments. The questions that should be asked include when did the need arise first, how did it arise, how was it being fulfilled till date, and how has the need changed over time. It is important to understand the needs to create a product that satisfies the customer.

#Why Study the History of the Industry and the Firms in it?

Studying the history of industries is important because it allows the analysts to understand the past, which in turn allows them to understand the present and strategise for the future in a better manner. To understand why the industry is the way it is, the history of the industry needs to be looked into. In business, it is often said, "History never repeats but it always rhymes." If analysts study the successes and failures of the past, they can avoid repeating many mistakes, as they know what works in any given industry.

The study of history of industry helps analysts and managers in the decision-making process. This happens in the following ways:

- **The ability to assess evidence and check assumptions:** The study of the industry's history builds experience in dealing with and assessing various kinds of evidence (different strategies and communications in the past). Analysts can use this evidence to put together the most accurate picture of the past and the present. They can also combine different kinds of evidence and make concrete arguments based on a variety of data. Such data-backed research allows the analysts to verify the correctness of the assumptions that they had made earlier. This forms the basis of various strategies they devise.[31]

- **Ability to assess conflicting interpretations:** Evaluating an industry's history means sorting through diverse and often conflicting interpretations regarding business models and value propositions. Examining past situations provides analysts the ability to be a critic of different approaches and understand the behaviour of the industry more objectively. It also aids the analysts in assessing conflicting interpretations and form a basis for one's own interpretations.[31]

- **Experience in assessing past examples of change:** Experience in assessing past examples of change is vital to understand changes in the industry today. Comparing particular changes with relevant examples from the past helps the analysts to understand the magnitude and significance of change. This in turn allows them to take decisions objectively.[31]

There is no exact science to understand the history and evolution of any given industry. There are a broad set of questions that can be asked, but everything boils down to understanding the origins of the industry and the way big companies have scaled up and why others have failed in the industry. The process requires intense reading of how various companies were started and their strategies over the years. This will

[31]   https://www.historians.org/about-aha-and-membership/aha-history-and-archives/historical-archives/why-study-history-(1998)

enable the analysts to draw conclusions about the evolution of the industry.

This is a broad, but not exhaustive, list of questions that should be asked to understand industry history and evolution.

- When was the need for the product first felt?

- What were the gains that the customers were trying to receive or the pains they were trying to relieve?

- Which was the first company started in the industry?

- How and when did the other companies start?

- Which are the companies that have gone on to become industry leaders?

- How were they established?

- When were they established?

- What strategies did they use for growing and scaling up their business?

- Which are the companies that started but have failed?

- Why did they fail?

- What strategies were they using for growth and scale-up?

- How has the need changed over time?

- How has the product changed over time?

- Is the history of the industry similar in other markets and geographies?

- How has government's attitude been towards the industry?

- What have been the biggest challenges for the industry over the years?

- How has the industry tried to solve them?

These questions together form the basis for reading and understanding the history and evolution of an industry and the firms in it.

Any analyst or entrepreneur planning to enter any sector must attempt to read about the history in order to strategise better for the future. This is one of the important points in the 9-point business circuit and it should not be ignored. Analysts and entrepreneurs often fall into the trap of ignoring this stage and they end up repeating the mistakes that were made earlier. For instance, many consumer electronic brands such as BPL, Micromax and Intex in India have had the same fate. They copied the Western players at a cheaper price point, sold to less demanding Indian masses and made a name for themselves. But when foreign players came at a lower price point or with more innovative products at low prices, the Indian firms found themselves at a position of disadvantage and were unable to maintain their position. Had these firms focussed on innovation from the beginning, they might have had different levels of success. For example, Symphony has long been able to maintain its leadership in the cooler industry globally by being innovative.

Logistics Industry History

- First serious logistics attempts were made during supplies of food, warfare material. They became critical factors behind winning and losing wars. Since then, logistics has evolved steadily and continued to remain critical over time.
- Railroads, steam engines, ships, automobiles followed by planes came to change the face of the logistics industry and started companies that we see today.
- As industries became larger and communication became easier, logistics companies could grow to a scale un-imagined before.
- Companies like FedEx, UPS, Nippon Express and DHL went on to become industry leaders.
- Most of these companies started early and, as industrial revolution caught up in those countries, they grew with them achieving economics of scale. Once they had scale, they could pick and choose new markets, and they began to dominate them over time.
- Others who had started failed because they could not achieve economics of scale.
- DHL started as a small company in the US but was bought over by Deutsche Post group. Post acquisition, it gained scale merits and access to Deutsche Post's transport network. So, it succeeded, capitalising on the opportunity using M&A.

- Nippon Express was started in 1872 and was mainly used for wartime material and personnel transport. That is where it got access to early scale advantages.
- XPO, STO, YTO and SFExpress are Chinese companies that grew with the support of Alibaba and Chinese e-commerce.
- FedEx began in 1971 and pioneered live tracking of packages, which instantly got it volumes. It capitalised on the advantage using M&A to gain scale benefits.
- Kuenhe - Nagel was used by the Nazis as an official transport company. Thus, it had early and exclusive access to scale.
- The product for such companies has evolved from majorly large B2B parcels to small B2C orders that need to be delivered to retail customers.
- The companies need quick, accessible and reliant logistic providers.
- The biggest challenge for the industry has been high operating leverage, high fleet and personnel maintenance.

Trends and Practices

Industry trends shed light on the direction in which the industry is moving. It helps in visualising the outcome of the industry. This is the fifth point of the 9-point business circuit and it focuses on the current state of the industry and the way things are done in the industry. It also focusses on the standard practices followed in the industry and the key changes that are underway. These practices can relate to any activity, big or small, in the industry and any vertical within the industry. It can also relate to the industry practices in marketing, product development and financing.

Defining 'industry practice' is difficult. One plausible definition is: An industry-accepted way of doing something that works. Let us work with this definition for now and proceed.

Industry practices can be divided into two: standard practices and best practices. As the name suggests, standard practice is the way most firms in the industry do things. Best practice is a method or technique that has consistently shown results superior to those achieved using other means.[32] Best practice can at times also be the most common practice used in the industry i.e. the standard practice in the industry.

---

[32]   https://judithcurry.com/2013/07/29/uncertainty-lost-in-translation/

It can be the practice used by most players in the industry or it can be something that is used only by a handful of players.

Both kind of practices can relate to any vertical in the industry. Standard practices and best practices relate to each activity in the value chain of the industry. An understanding of value chain from the first tier of the broad industry analysis would help in understanding the industry practices. Value chain deals with 'what is being done' whereas industry practices deals with 'how it is being done'. The benefit with standard and best practices in the industry is that they are already being deployed by other players and the results are known, expected and tested in the market. There is evidence that a particular practice actually works and will produce results.

The problem with best practices and standard practices is the same as their benefits – they are being done by other players and the results are known and expected. As other players are already practising them, these firms enjoy an early-mover advantage. Hence, new firms stand at a position of disadvantage. Also, the result is known and expected by all. Starting such a business or investing in one that follows all the industry standard practices is a definite way to create a 'me too' business wherein the profitability would always be under threat from direct competition.

So, why should the entrepreneur understand the industry practices? Simply because it gives him decision-making power—to decide the activities to go with the industry and the areas to go against the industry, where to defy the best practices/standard practices and try something of his own, in which the result may be unknown to others. It allows the entrepreneur a source of potential differentiation in the major activities of the value chain, which are critical to success. This can save him the hassle of reinventing the wheel for less critical activities in the value chain activities. Firms can stick to industry practices in areas that are less critical for success. This would save them time and effort and also give some predictability of the outcomes.

Knowledge of industry practices—how things are being done in the industry—saves the entrepreneur and business manager from creating a 'me too' company and a product and allows them a chance to stand out in the industry. However, the potential outcome of defying best practices is unknown. Hence, this can be costly as well as risky for the firm. It may cause failure but it also has a potential of a much higher return if the approach works. It may even see others shifting to this new 'best practice' and starting at a position of relative disadvantage.

It is important for the investor to be aware of how things are being done in the industry, so that he knows what to expect from different players who are following different practices. This knowledge gives the investor the ability to spot firms within the industry that are doing things differently. Knowledge of industry practices allows the investor to be a much active participant in the company's decision-making process. It also allows the investor to comprehend management communication and future strategies in a much better manner.

As a result, it can be concluded that knowledge of how things are done complements the knowledge of what things are being done. Knowing about the value chain is very important for both the entrepreneur as well as the investor.

Knowledge of how things are being done (industry practices) involves answering questions such as these:

- How is the hiring done in the industry?

- How are the employees trained?

- How are technology upgradations installed?

- What software does the industry use for its operations?

- How does the R&D department work?

- What is the product innovation process?

- How are the raw materials procured?

- How is logistics done?

- How is warehousing of raw materials and finished products done?

- What manufacturing process is being used? What technology is being used?

- How are marketing and sales done?

- How is after-sales service provided?

- How is feedback collected from customers?

The above questions are sample questions that allow an understanding of industry practices. The list by no means is exhaustive. 'How' questions can be asked for almost every activity done by the firms in an industry. The entrepreneur or business manager should try and identify critical activities for success in the industry through a thorough reading of industry's history and try doing things differently. However, this should not be done merely for the sake of being a contrarian in the industry. The attempt must be backed by proper research and logic.

Major Practices in Logistics Industry

Major industry practices include:

- Renting the warehouses instead of owning them
- Owning the warehouse equipment, designed by the company at times
- Owning a small part of the fleet while outsourcing major requirements
- Asset-light model to scale the business
- Building multi-modal networks for logistics
- Working based on collaborations, particularly by smaller players

The players can decide based on strategic planning that they wish to follow industry practices or defy them and try to create a source of differentiation.

#Trends in the Industry

A trend, in general, refers to the general direction in which something is developing or changing. In the business scenario, an industry trend refers to the direction in which any industry is moving or the way in which it is developing. Industry trends are examined to foresee what the industry should look like in the future and to make predictions. These trends could relate to consumer behaviour, employment, technological advancements, new product development, competition, and government norms.[33]

Understanding the industry trends is important to a company's success and significance. It foretells the future and also impacts the present. Trends help an investor and entrepreneur decide if an industry is worth entering. However, one thing to be kept in mind is that the industry trends are not fads that come and go. They are generally sustainable and long-term routes that the industry takes and there is generally no going back once the industry adopts them.

Trends determine how the industry shall look in the future. This allows business managers and entrepreneurs to be prepared and position themselves in the industry in such a way that they benefit when the time comes, rather than stand at a position of disadvantage. They can participate in the change that happens and benefit when it gets bigger. Also, trends help investor identify areas of interest and areas from which they should stay away. A correct understanding of trends helps gain insights about the industry and its future.

The real challenge when foreseeing the future of an industry is identifying which changes are one-time changes and which ones are more structural. Only the structural changes are copied by others and they go on to become current industry trends. If an entrepreneur or investor picks up the wrong changes as trends, his vision for the future of the industry may be very different from the reality and it may take him along a different path, which can even turn out to be punishing in the future.

Many successful businesses were started by entrepreneurs who had the ability to spot trends before anyone else. They were able to capitalise on their insights in a new and creative way.

---

[33]   https://www.financialexpress.com/opinion/explained-the-difference-between-sector-and-industry/1349168/

Thus, efforts to identify new changes affecting the industry and the direction in which the industry is moving can not only save firms from losses but also help them stay better prepared when the time for change comes. Efforts and resources should be allocated to such trend-spotting.

To sum it up, the fourth stage deals with trends and practices in the industry. The practices deal with how things are done in the industry and they help decide where to deviate from standard practices in order to create a potential source of differentiation. Trends focus on identifying the changes in the industry early on, in order to prepare for them and face them as opportunities rather than challenges.

Major Trends affecting logistics industry in India

Major trends that are affecting the logistics segment include:

- Focus on automation
- Asset-light model
- Focus on technological advancements in various fields relating to logistics
- Modern warehouses over traditional warehouses
- Multi-modal integrated network
- Extended use of 3PL services by different sectors
- Last-mile delivery innovations
- Focus on data analytics
- Making the logistics network more flexible and adaptive

Investors as well as business analysts must be on the lookout to see how these trends would affect the industry going forward and how they can benefit from them.

Risks and Growth Potential

The sixth point in the 9-point business circuit is risks and growth potential. This point relates to both the industry-level analysis as well as the business level analysis. At the industry level, industry-specific factors that determine the risks and growth potential of the industry are considered. At the firm level, company-specific factors are also considered. The focus at this step is on industry-specific risks and the industry's growth potential.

Risks related to industry have already been covered in the second stage of the broad industry analysis in the first tier. Risks associated with the industry must be revisited to sharpen the understanding after collection of new information in the various stages of the 9-point analysis. The purpose is to make sure that any major risk relating to the industry does not go unnoticed.

We can conclude the industry analysis by trying to understand its growth potential. The goal is to understand how firms grow in the industry and how the overall industry grows. The overall industry growth is what determines the potential market size (this was covered in the second tier of the broad industry analysis). It depends on factors such as:

- Population size

- Penetration rate

- Adoption ratio

- More uses of the same product

- Formalisation of the industry

After finishing all the steps in the industry analysis, analysts and entrepreneurs should revisit the risks and growth potential while making a decision to enter the industry. Risks relate to what could go against them in the industry. Also, a favourable growth outlook for the overall industry is good news for any firm operating in it. These two factors are crucial before making the final decision to enter the industry.

Risks and growth need a balance between them. A too-risky business with high growth prospects may not be the best choice for an entrepreneur or investor. Similarly, a very poor growth potential but low risks will also be unattractive to many. A balance is needed between growth and risks.

The fifth stage is the last stage in conducting any industry analysis. At this stage, enough information has been collected in a structured manner. This information will enable any entrepreneur or investor to decide rationally whether to enter the industry or not. The remaining points in the 9-point business circuit deal with aspects such as company-specific factors, company's financial performance, and management incentives. These shall be discussed in subsequent books.

14-Day Plan

14-Day Plan to Industry Research

We have discussed the factors affecting any particular industry and its attractiveness in the chapters earlier. Now, analysts, entrepreneurs and investors need to put these analytical models into action. It is however, easy to get lost about where to begin when actually applying these models. So, a 14-day plan has been developed to have a decisive understanding of the industry.

The plan is said to be a 14- day plan because that is the ideal time to have a good understanding of the industry with reasonable depth. However, the tenure of the analysis can be extended or reduced based on the scope of industry research, purpose of analysis and level of depth required. For instance, investors benefit from diversification and can thus take a decisive call about the industry after 14–21 days of research. However, for entrepreneurs, the level of depth required is much higher as they do not benefit from diversification. So, a period of 30–45 days can be applied to get a complete and decisive understanding of the industry. In some cases this period can be even longer. Remember, the purpose is to have a decisive understanding of the industry's attractiveness and then to make incremental commitments if the analysis holds true. The 14-day plan is not to stop the analyst from further incremental learning;

that is a process that will go on. The objective, at the end of 14 days, is to create an 'industry sheet' for a particular segment. (Industry sheet has been introduced in the next chapter.)

Day 1

On day 1, analysts may have some knowledge about the industry from prior experience or no knowledge at all. If there is some prior knowledge, the challenge is to check the correctness of the knowledge and structure it over the 14 days so that decision-making can be facilitated.

On day 1, analysts must begin by developing some background for the industry. This begins with reading the secondary research available on the industry on the internet. The reading materials include industry reports by consultancy firms like Bain & Co, BCG, McKinsey and KPMG and industry authorities like FICCI and CII. Reports by government authorities can also be read. Reports by private industry research firms like IBEF also provide good insights.

Reports by brokerage firms should be ignored at this stage of analysis as they are opinionated.

This preliminary reading allows analysts to have some understanding of the industry's products, customers, variables and trends.

On day 1, analysts must try to understand the different segments of the market and how customers can be segmented. Active effort should be put on identifying the various basis of segmentation that can be used in the industry.

Day 1 gives a brief background about the industry. Even though it is unstructured initially, it will act as a base for reading in the coming days. Also, identification of customer segments is obtained on day 1.

Day 2 and Day 3

Once the customers have been identified, time must be spent on understanding the customers. Remember, in business as well as in investing, when in doubt, ask the customers. Customers are the ultimate authorities who decide the success and failure of any business. So, time must be spent on understanding the gains and pains of the customers and creating the customer profile. The functional, psychological and social pains and gains shall all be identified in this phase.

The problem here is time. Two days is too less a time to establish a concrete customer profile for each of the customer segments identified. As a result, a few things need to be kept in mind. Firstly, the scope of the customer segments needs to be identified to narrow down on a few segments that are relevant to the purpose of analysis. The segments selected should be profiled actively.

Also, it is important to understand that the purpose of the 14-day plan is to do a decisive screening of whether to enter the industry or not. From past experience, it is believed that enough understanding is established in two days to know about the pains and gains of the customers in the industry. For a more detailed understanding, more time and resources are committed to customer profiling once the entry decision has been made. But, at this stage, resources have not yet been committed.

Customer profiling is something that investors and business managers need to do across the life of the company and the industry. Customers keep changing and so should their profile, for businesses to stay relevant.

Here, customers should be first understood based on secondary reading and listening to the videos of industry experts. However, more time should be spent on understanding the customers through primary research. Talking to distribution channels, sales representatives and customers themselves would give amazing insights. If customers cannot be reached physically, even phone calls work wonders. Around 100 phone calls over two days to a well-spread-out sample have the ability to yield conclusive evidence about customer behaviour. Other than the pains and gains, the focus here is also on understanding the purchase and consumption behaviour of the customers.

One must not rush through this step; it must be done very carefully. A poorly made customer profile would cause all other analysis efforts to be irrelevant. If the customer segments are many or confidence is not established over the customer profile, analysts must consider spending one more day over the customer profile, making it a 15-day plan.

Day 4

The entire day must be spent identifying and understanding all the different products and services being offered by various players in the industry. The features of all the products should be known; how they relieve various pains and create various gains must be understood. Focus should also be paid to substitute industries as they too are competing for the same customers.

All products would have different features and different versions. The focus is to understand which gains and pains of the customers are being served and which ones are being ignored. This gives an entrepreneur an opportunity to start serving those needs. Analysts would have an understanding of how the industry is working and what blind spots it has. Understanding customers and the matching products and services helps establish the value proposition for the industry. How the value is being created and delivered can be understood. Value propositions of various substitute industries can be compared.

Day 5

Now that enough time has been spent understanding the customers and the value proposition of the industry, begin understanding the structure of the industry. On day 5, a value chain is created for the industry. It will help identify the critical activities for success. This will allow the investor to know which activities to compare. This will allow business managers to decide which industries require greater focus.

The data can be collected by speaking to various players in the industry or through secondary sources. If a visit to any of the players in the industry, no matter how small they are, can be arranged, it would help understand the value chain in a much better manner.

This day would also focus on creating the industry map. This again can be created with the help of conversations with industry experts as well as looking into the secondary resources available.

Day 6

Day 6 continues with understanding the profit pool of the industry. Creation of profit pool has been discussed in the previous sections. Profit pool would help identify the activities that make the highest profitability.

A major part of this day should, however, be spent on understanding the demand-supply scenario, adhering to the laws of economics. The demand-supply balance determines the industry's profitability. From past experience, it is understood that secondary research is much more productive and effective while estimating the demand-supply scenario. Data could be obtained from secondary sources and then conclusions can be drawn. The conclusions can then be verified by conversations with industry players and experts to get clues on the tone of the industry. The tone of the industry will help identify if the analysis is in the right direction.

Day 7

Day 7 begins with analysing the industry size and the potential size in a few years. Secondary sources should be used for this.

The next step, on this day, is to identify the degree of industrial stability. Market shares of various firms are calculated over time to recognise the industry stability.

Lastly, pricing power of the industry is understood. Quantity and price behaviour of individual companies in the industry is understood. However, there may be issues regarding information availability at this stage. General conversations with industry experts should help clear these ambiguities. One must not consider the pricing power of the few big players alone to generalise the power of the entire industry. Pricing power with smaller companies should be looked into as well.

Day 8

Day 8 focusses on understanding the stage of the competitive life cycle the industry is in. It focusses on identifying the characteristics of various firms in the industry and then deciding the stage at which the industry is currently operating. Understanding the life cycle stage helps establish the kind of strategies and financial performance that can be expected by the industry.

This day is slightly light with some spare time, in order to complete any incomplete steps from the previous days.

The research must be fine-tined. Concrete research would act as a base for good decision-making.

Day 9

Day 9 is a very critical day as it helps understand the constraints of the industry set by the government. All governmental laws and regulations about the industry are understood on this day. Various kinds of laws, acts and taxes help understand what the government thinks about the industry and what their approach is towards policy-making for the industry.

Government regulations relating to any particular industry are generally difficult to find through secondary sources. Here, two methods seem to work. First—talking to industry participants. As they already are operating in the industry, they are well-versed with the various laws affecting the industry. Second—going to various ministries and industry portals where notifications and circulars about the industry are updated. These portals generally have detailed documents about various laws affecting the industry. However, these require a thorough reading of the fine print to understand the laws. Without knowledge of the laws affecting the industry, one simply cannot operate or invest in the industry. Another way to know the laws, although it is expensive, is to meet a legal counsel or a compliance officer catering to firms in that particular industry.

Day 10

Day 10 focusses on identifying the influence of Porter's five forces model. Enough information has been collected in the previous days; so analysts would be in a position to assess the influence of individual factors. Discussions with industry participants can also help understand the influence better.

Once the effect of individual factors has been established, the effect of each of the forces on the profitability of industry can be understood.

The current as well as potential profitability and attractiveness of the industry can be understood using the five forces model.

Day 11

On day 11, analysts must focus on the quantitative performance of the various firms in the industry. A sample of firms (minimum 3) must be selected and their financial performance over the past few years is established. This does not include a very detailed analysis of the financials but includes various important financial metrics. Return attractiveness is analysed through return on equity analysis and DuPont analysis.

Furthermore, growth and investment needs of the firms in the industry are understood. Once these are understood for the sample firms, generalised conclusions about the industry can be drawn from the same.

Day 12

Day 12 is spent on identifying and understanding the trends in the industry. The developing trends around the industry will determine the direction the industry will take. Attention is paid to conversations on various forums and what industry experts have to say. In practice, one tends to put in more focus on what practitioners say over what external analysts say. This helps put the industry outlook in perspective. Investors and practitioners must identify the forces that they need to keep an eye on. Trends in not just the domestic market of the industry but other markets too should be studied.

Day 13

This day, in my opinion, is the most critical day of the entire process. This day focusses on identifying and understanding the potential risk factors. These factors will determine the attractiveness of the industry in the true sense. A very risky industry would generally have a very attractive structure. But the risks involved in pursuing that industry make it much less attractive.

So, proper attention should be paid to identify the various risk sources. Techniques to identify and analyse the risks have been discussed in the previous chapters.

Day 14

The last day of the analysis includes identifying the growth factors of the industry. This stage is kept at the end because it is very easy to get biased if an industry has a very high growth outlook. The various factors of growth will determine the rate at which the firms in the industry can grow year on year.

Finally, once the analysts have completed the 14 days, a good understanding of the industry is gained.

Even though, by this time, analysts would have gained personal biases to like or dislike the industry, it is important for them to think objectively and decide whether the industry is worth investing. The above exercise will give entrepreneurs an objective picture of whether to pursue an idea or not. The purpose here is not to give a complete understanding of the industry. Incremental learning would go on for a lifelong term. The focus here is to build a strong and structured foundation, over which great investments and businesses can be built, on the back of solid research.

Industry Sheet, Qualitatives and Conclusion

Once the five points of the 9-point business circuit, which relates to the industry analysis, have been discussed and understood, they can be together used to form what is called an 'industry sheet'.

The 'industry sheet' along with 'business sheet' and 'management sheet' (which shall be introduced in other books) form what are called 'Qualitatives'. Just like how balance sheet, income statement and cash flow statement form the 'financials' of a company and together help understand the financial strength and performance of a company, similarly 'qualitatives' are designed to understand the fundamental strength and performance of industries and the companies operating in them.

The Purpose of the Sheets

Industry sheet: To identify the industries that are inherently more attractive than others. Industry sheets compare various industries on common grounds and help identify the stronger or more attractive ones.

Business sheet: To identify companies that are better placed than their competitors in the industry. It helps identify companies that have a 'right to win'. It discusses the business model of the companies, differentiation drivers and cost drivers. These together help identify the best-placed company.

Management sheet: Management sheet is inspired by what is called the 'VMI' model. It helps identify the vision, motivation and integrity of the management. It deals with identifying the management's vision with the business. Motivation helps identify how motivated the management is and if its interest is in line with the shareholders. Integrity is far more subjective and very difficult to evaluate than the other factors. However, parts of the management sheet indicate the management's commitment to firm goals and thus integrity.

Like financials, qualitatives can also be used to compare. They can be used to compare factors across industries, companies and economies. They can also be used to compare different timeframes – over years – to see how industries/companies have evolved and identify the changes that have occurred. Qualitatives can also help screen ideas.

Like financials, qualitatives also enhance 'understandability'. They provide information that is readily understandable to the users of qualitative statements. This means data is clearly presented, with additional information supplied as supporting footnotes, as needed, to assist in clarification. Thus, qualitatives give a snap view of the company and industry with detailed explanation in the footnotes.[34]

However, qualitatives are different from financials in one major aspect. Qualitatives are much more subjective than financials. This is because financials only include numbers and quantitative expression. However, qualitatives can use both numbers as well as descriptions. Also, qualitatives do not have a system of double-entry to balance

---

[34]   http://accountingtools1.squarespace.com/questions-and-answers/?currentPage=1088

entries. Besides these, qualitatives stand true on all characteristics of financials.

This book particularly talks about the industry and thus introduces the industry sheet and the industry sheet template. Its application in various industries has also been shown. These are 'at-a-point-in-time' applications and are not comparative as of now. As there is no database of such an industry sheet in the past, there is an absence of reference to compare with. Going ahead, the analyst must update the industry sheet every year to identify new developments. With a gap of few years, the industry sheet can be compared with past sheets to identify how the industry has changed.

Industry Sheet

For XYZ Industry

As on xx / xx / xxxx

Factors	Note	Particulars
1. Value Proposition		
Customer segments		who, when, where, what, why
Customer gains		required, desired, unexpected gains
Customer pains		pains, risks
Products and services		features, pain relievers, gain creators
2. Activities and Participants		
Value chain		direct activities, support activities
Industry map		suppliers, external forces, middlemen, customers
Profit pool		segment-wise ROI, revenue
Demand-supply scenario		demand, supply, capacity utilisation

3. Industry Characteristics		
Market size study		size, growth
Industry stability		market share
Pricing power		price, volume
Competitive life cycle		stage, characteristics
Disruptions threat		sustaining, low end, new market
Regulations		taxes and duties, legal acts, ownership related, industry-specific
4. Profit Forces		
Supplier power		
Buyer power		
Threat of substitution		
Threat of entry		
Competitive rivalry in the industry		
5. Financial Health		
ROE and DuPont analysis		PAT margin, asset turnover, leverage
Growth		PAT growth, revenue growth
Investment needs		FCF, fixed investment, working capital investment
6. Outlook		
Trends in industry		same market, different markets
Industry-specific risks		
Growth factors		
Variables for success in industry		

Industry Sheet

For Indian Private Dairy Industry

As on 30/06/2019

Factors	Note	Particulars
1. Value Proposition		
Customer segments	1	• Urban and rural markets • B2B and B2C
Customer gains	2,3,4	• Clean and fresh • Nutrition value • Consistency • New products • Regular supply • Price
Customer pains	2,3,4	• Adulteration • Inconsistent products • Irregular supply • Logistic issues Door delivery
Products and services	2,3,4	liquid milk, butter, ghee, paneer, cheese, value-added products
2. Activities and Participants		
Value chain	5	Key activities • Farmer procurement • Transport to village milk collection centre • Transport to milk processing unit • Processed and packaged • Distribution channels • Brand building activities

Industry map	6	Key players: farmers, agents, logistics partners, distributors, retail players, FSSAI
Profit pool	7	Activities in order of attractiveness: milk, curd, paneer, ghee, cheese
Demand-supply scenario	8	Seasonality in milk production; low in summer months • 2000 - 78 mn MT • 2010 - 116 mn MT • 2017 - 169 mn MT • 2020E - 188 mn MT • 2027E - 244 mn MT
3. Industry Characteristics		
Market size study	9	Total milk production - $107 bn Self-consumption - $58 bn Surplus sold - $49 bn Unorganised - $34 bn Organised - $15 bn
Industry stability		Amul has been the leader for decades in the cooperative sector. Private players have slowly gained and maintained share. Thus, it is a stable industry.
Pricing power		Cooperatives set the selling prices. Thus, private players have no pricing power.
Competitive life cycle		Milk is at growth stage; premium products are at growth stage.
Disruptions threat		There is no disruption threat. There is sustaining innovation with value-added products.

Regulations		• FSSAI • Ministry of Animal Husbandry • National Dairy Development Board of India
4. Profit Forces		
Supplier power	10	High
Buyer power	11	Low
Threat of substitution	12	Low
Threat of entry	13	Moderate
Competitive rivalry in the industry	14	Moderate (healthy)
5. Financial Health		
ROE and DuPont analysis (PAT margin x Operating asset t/o x Leverage)	15	• Parag Milk Foods(FY19) - 5% x 3.5x x 1x = 17.5% • Hatsun Agro - 2.8% x 3x x 2x = 16.8% • Heritage Foods - 3.2% x 4.x 0.7x = 9.4% The industry is a low-margin, moderately-high-turnover business.
Growth	16	• Parag Milk Foods (5-yr CAGR) PAT – 49.32%, Revenue – 17.10% • Hatsun Agro (5yr CAGR) PAT – 9.07%, Revenue – 13.81% • Heritage Foods PAT – 12.61%, Revenue – 7.87% The firms in the industry have been growing at low teens.

Investment needs	17	• Parag Milk - Regular Fixed and W/c investment • Hatsun Agro – Very high fixed capital investment • Hatsun – High fixed capital investment Thus, the industry shows high capital investment.
6. Outlook		
Trends in industry	18, 19, 20	• Rise of private players • Direct procurement from farmers – no agents • Companies have grown through M&A of regional companies • Increased focus on nutrition by customers
Industry-specific risks		• Selling prices determined by cooperatives • Supply issue with raw milk • Difficulty in getting distribution space • SMP price fluctuations • Changes in customer behaviour

Growth factors		<ul><li>Vegetarian population with protein deficiency</li><li>Rising share of organised sector</li><li>Faster growth in value-added products</li><li>Premiumisation</li><li>Westernisation of meals</li><li>Increase in eating-out population</li></ul>
Variables for success in industry		<ul><li>Procurement network stable</li><li>Product mix (value-added products)</li><li>Distribution strength</li><li>Manufacturing distribution</li><li>Branding</li></ul>

Notes

On the basis of 'where' it is consumed and typical behaviour of consumers there – Urban and Rural

On the basis of 'who' is the buyer – B2B and B2C

1. Urban buyers - customer profile

Gains

Required gains

- Cleanliness and freshness

- Nutrition

- Uninterrupted supply

Desired gains

- New flavours and varieties in milk production
- Consistency in quality
- Consistency in food products
- Approval by food authorities

Unexpected gains

- Door delivery
- High shelf life

Pains

- Inconsistent products
- Adulterated with preservatives
- Lack of regularity
- Non-accessibility

Products and services – liquid milk, ghee, paneer, cheese, butter

Pain relievers

- FSSAI approved products
- Distribution through mom and pop stores, retail supermarkets and milkmen

Gain creators

- FSSAI
- New product innovations
- Quality maintenance due to regulatory monitoring

2. Rural customers – customer profile

Gains

Required gains

- Cleanliness and freshness
- Nutrition

Desired gains

- Fresh products
- Home processes milk products (not factory-processed)
- High fat content

Unexpected gains

- Door delivery

Pains

- Adulterated milk
- Lack of regular supply
- Low shelf life

Pain relievers

- Higher shelf life of products

Gain creators

- Availability in mom and pop stores

(As a result, private companies mainly focus on more-demanding urban consumers who are willing to pay a premium.)

3. B2B (hotels, restaurants, QSRs, food packages, etc.)

Gains

Required gains

- Consistency in quality
- Cost conscious

Desired gains

- Branded products for consistency across its chain
- Regular availability
- Value-added products

Unexpected gains

- High shelf life in inventory
- Logistics convenient packaging

Pains

- Lack of regular supply in required quantity
- Logistics issues

Pain relievers

- SMPs procured for regular supply
- Focus on shelf life

Gain creators

- New product innovations
- FSSAI approved
- Consistent procurement from similar cattle for consistency

B2C customers: They are divided into urban and rural customers and have customer profile as discussed above.

4. Industry value chain

Infrastructure	production site maintenance, production site audit, refer truck network management
HRM	product development scientists, sales representatives, marketing professionals, compensation structuring
R&D	new product development, approvals to produce (FSSAI), focus on increasing shelf life
Procurement	through farmers, running village level milk collection centres, agents, farmer community building, farmer relationship management
Inbound logistics	bulk milk coolers, large milk chilling centres, transportation network to transport raw milk
Operations	milk filtering, milk segregation, packaging raw milk, conversion to value-added products, conversion to SMP (surplus)
Outbound logistics	transportation network
Marketing and sales	dealer network management, retailer network management, brand building activities, advertisements, sales reps, reach expansion
Service	customer feedback, retail feedback

(These are the key activities that need to be done by anyone who wishes to start a business in the dairy industry.)

5. Industry map

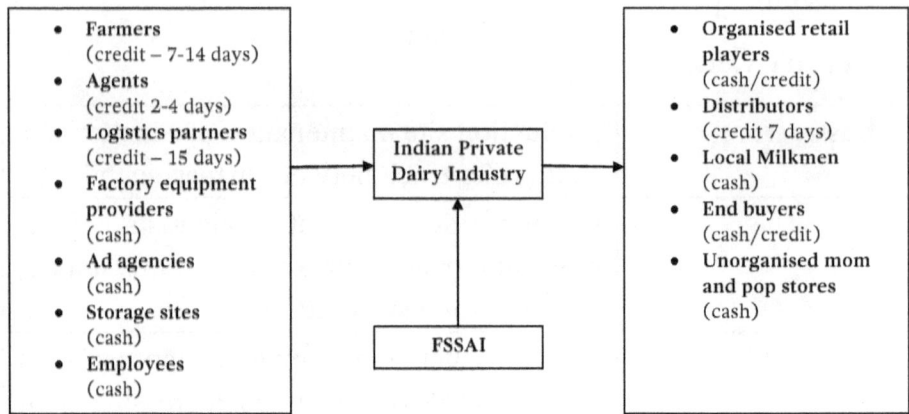

6. Profit pool

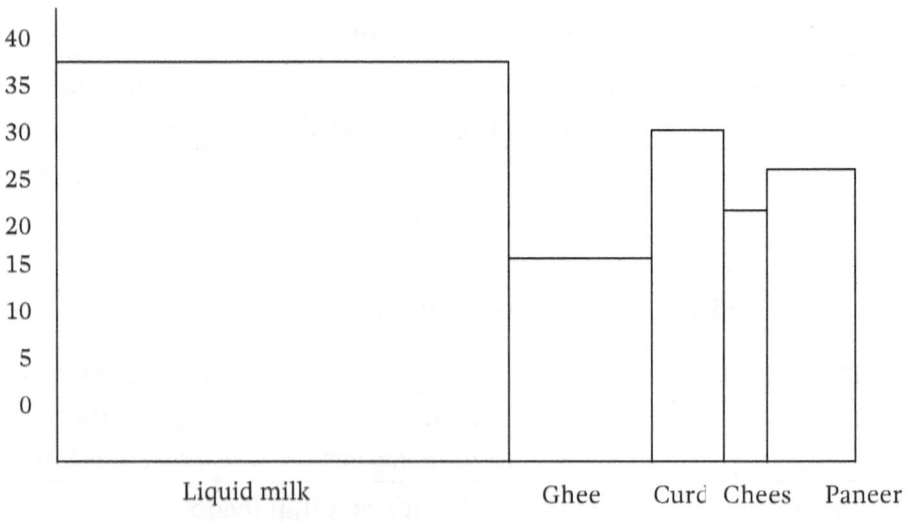

Product market size

7.

Year	Production (mn MT)
1950	17
1970	21
1990	51
2010	116
2017	168
2020E	188
2027E	244

(Source: Ministry of Animal Husbandry, Dairy and Fisheries)

8. Market size

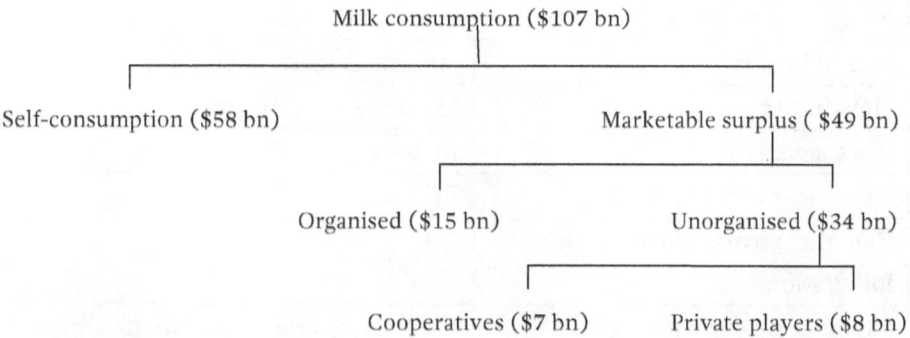

(Source: PPFAS presentation on YouTube – Understanding dairy industry in India)

9. Supplier power

Number of suppliers in market	Many farmers but often unionised
Availability of regular supply	Moderate for established firms
Uniqueness of services	No substitute
Ability to substitute	No substitute

Switching costs	High cost and effort to set up new procurement network
Dependency of industry on them	Moderate dependency
Can the industry threaten to vertically integrate?	No
Importance of volume to supplier's profitability	No
Payment power with the supplier	Cash or credit up to 14 days

Supplier power is present if the farmers are unionised. In reality, farmers are only unionised at the community level, thus resulting in moderate supplier power.

10. Buyer power

Number of buyers/customers	Mass-market product
Size of buyers/orders	Small and scattered orders
How informed are the buyers?	Moderately informed
Price sensitivity	Inelastic
Demand- supply scenario	Balance
Can the buyers threaten vertical integration?	No
Payment power with buyers	Cash sales; some credit to distributors

There is no buyer power. There is very low buyer power with intermediaries. This cannot affect profitability though.

11. Threat of substitution

Availability of substitute to the goods	No substitute (Horlicks is a very distant substitutes)
Ability to substitute	No substitute
Cost of switching	No substitute
Price performance of substitute vs the industry	No substitute

12. Threat of entry

Time and cost of sizeable entry	Time and cost is high
Economics of scale	High economies of scale (marketing and distribution)
Distribution strength required	High
Cost advantages to existing players	Yes; access to farmers for procurement
Switching costs for customers	Habit
Asset specificity in the industry	Geographic asset specificity
Proprietary product difference	Medium for value-added products; low for milk
Network effect of the product	No
Protection against new entrants	No
Brand identity	High
Reputation of existing firms	Moderately important for sales
Response by incumbents on new entry	Moderate Strategic response

New entry takes time to build. However, firms can enter the industry using pre-established brands.

13. Competitive rivalry

Number of competitors in the industry	A few (geography-wise micro markets matter)
How concentrated is the industry	Moderately dilute
Differences in product quality	Minor difference in liquid milk
Cost of switching products	Habit
Is the industry growing?	Moderate growth
Overcapacity in the industry	Seasonal
Fixed costs in the industry	Medium
Exit barriers in the industry	Low
Basis of competition in the industry	Competition based on advertising and new products

Low competitive rivalry exists. Competition is favourable as price competition is not too high. Basis of competition allows the industry to grow.

14. Return on equity and DuPont analysis

Parag Milk Foods

	2015	2016	2017	2018	2019
PAT margin	2.21%	2.29%	0.31%	4.45%	5.04%
Asset turnover	3.06x	2.44x	2.81x	2.57x	2.86x
Leverage	3.8	1.87	0.98	1.07	1.02
ROE	25.69%	10.45%	0.86%	12.24%	14.62%
ROA	23.94%	22.37%	14.91%	25.92%	26.84%
Dividend payout	0%	0%	88%	7%	7%
SGR	25.69%	10.45%	0.11%	11.42%	13.82%

Heritage Foods

	2015	2016	2017	2018	2019
PAT margin	1.35%	2.31%	3.16%	2.65%	3.22%
Asset turnover	5.69x	6.09x	5.38x	4.66x	4.44x
Leverage	1.89	1.63	0.59	0.65	0.71
ROE	14.52%	22.93%	10.04%	8.03%	10.15%
ROA	23.07%	33.76%	38.76%	-50.9%	10.07%
Dividend payout	25%	13%	3%	15%	11%
SGR	10.89%	19.94%	9.7%	6.8%	8.9%

Hatsun Agro

	2015	2016	2017	2018	2019
PAT margin	1.33%	1.74%	3.21%	2.12%	2.42%
Asset turnover	3.70x	3.98x	3.66x	3.07x	2.99x
Leverage	3.57	3.74	3.29	3.83	1.97
ROE	17.56%	25.9%	38.65%	24.92%	13.82%
ROA	24.96%	35.2%	33.01%	26.62%	28.17%
Dividend payout	0%	0%	88%	7%	7%
SGR	25.69%	10.45%	0.11%	11.42%	13.82%

15. PAT and revenue growth

Parag Milk Foods	2015	2016	2017	2018	2019
Revenue Growth	32.6%	13.99%	5.22%	12.9%	22.5%
PAT growth	100%	46.8%	-87%	1700% (Base year)	39.1%

Hatsun Agro	2015	2016	2017	2018	2019
Revenue Growth	17.6%	17.6%	21.8%	2.1%	11.04%
PAT growth	-52%	53.8%	125%	-27.2%	26.37%

Heritage Foods	2015	2016	2017	2018	2019
Revenue Growth	20.38%	14.86%	-21%	25.29%	5.9%
PAT growth	-37%	95%	24%	5%	28.57%

16. Investment needs

Parag Milk Foods	2015	2016	2017	2018	2019
CFO	88	59	(17)	19	140
Fixed Investment	(30)	(27)	(94)	(63)	(85)
FCF	58	22	(111)	(44)	55
Revenue	1443	1645	1731	1955	2396

Hatsun Agro	2015	2016	2017	2018	2019
CFO	62	219	433	277	375
Fixed Investment	(128)	(140)	(573)	(532)	(351)
FCF	(66)	79	(140)	(255)	24
Revenue	2933	3445	4198	4287	4760

Heritage Foods	2015	2016	2017	2018	2019
CFO	52	125	115	121	148
Fixed Investment	(51)	(68)	(93)	(144)	(127)
FCF	1	57	22	(23)	21
Revenue	2073	2381	1894	2373	2515

17. **Rise of private players (benefits for farmers)**

- No concept of milk holidays: During surplus production, cooperatives used to refuse milk from farmers. These periods of overproduction were milk holidays. Private players did not do so.

- Higher realisation v/s cooperatives: As private players could also charge higher charges against the cooperatives due to their brand.

- Transparency and timeliness in payments

- Support services to farmers (E.g. credit, cattle feed)

- More efficiently managed

19. **Advantages of direct procurement from farmers**

- Elimination of agent commission

- Lower working capital investments: Farmers are paid once a week v/s agents paid every two days.

- Much higher stability of supply: Agents may switch to supply to rival firms.

- Greater proximity to farmers: Farmers get better support as well.

Challenges of direct procurement

- Best producing areas near metros are already occupied by existing companies.

- It is difficult to make the farmer switch to a new company as they trust the older ones.

20. Indian companies growing through mergers and acquisitions

- Hindustan Unilever acquired Adityaa in Karnataka in August 2017.

- Heritage Foods acquired Varman Milk in Punjab in November 2017.

- Lactalis acquired Tirumala in Andhra Pradesh in January 2017.

- Parag Milk Foods acquired Danone's plant in April 2018 for access to northern India.

21. History of dairy sector in India

- In 1946, dairy farmers in Anand, Gujarat formed their own cooperative to fight against unfair trade practices of middlemen.

- In 1970, Operation Flood was implemented.

- In 1991, the dairy sector was deregulated and privatised.

- In 2003, milk and milk products order was amended. Private companies did not have to register with local authorities. They were granted complete autonomy.

- India turned from a milk deficit country to a milk surplus country between 1970 and 1990.

Industry Sheet

For Indian Premier League Franchisees

As on 30/10/2019

Factors	Note	Particulars
1. Value Proposition		
Customer segments	1	Viewers, Advertisers
Customer gains	2, 3	Viewers • Entertainment • Sense of belonging Advertisers • Business growth • Brand building • Customer awareness
Customer pains	2, 3	Viewers • Expensive forms of entertainment otherwise • Peer pressure Advertisers • Lack of events with high viewership • Expensive ad rates • Lack of consistency in ad platforms
Products and services		• Matches • Fan parks • Events about the matches • Merchandise • Ad space for advertisers • On-ground campaigns

2. Activities and Participants		
Value chain	4	Key activities • Player management • Ground Management • Analytics • Sponsorship procurement • Media advertisements and brand building • Logistics and administrative issues
Industry map	5	Key players • Players • Support staff • BCCI • Broadcasters • Sponsors • Audience
Demand-supply scenario	6	462 million TV viewers for IPL 2019 (Up 12% y-o-y) Rs 2100 crore for Sony (broadcasters) – TV ad collection in 2019
3. Industry Characteristics		
Market size study	7	• IPL 2018–22 rights value at Rs 16,347 cr by Start India • Favourable demand supply. • Next auction due in 2022 for 2023–27
Industry stability	8	No new teams being launched; each team maintaining share; thus, a stable industry
Pricing power		Auction format for pricing of sponsorship fees; thus, no exercise of pricing power

Competitive life cycle		• Mature stage • Teams easily finding sponsors • Viewership steady
Disruptions threat	9	Distant threat of new market disruption by other port leagues E.g. Pro Kabaddi, ISL, HIL
Regulations		• No specific government regulations • IPL governing body to be followed by teams • BCCI guidelines to be followed • Supreme Court appointed COA • IPL rules and guidelines
4. Profit Forces		
Supplier power	10	Moderate
Buyer power	11	Low
Threat of substitution	12	Low
Threat of entry	13	Low
Competitive rivalry in the industry	14	Low
5. Financial Health		
ROE and DuPont analysis		• CSK – ROE – 91% • PAT margin – 26% • The companies have no leverage and negligible asset requirements.
Growth		Major growth comes every 5 years when broadcast rights are re-auctioned.
Investment needs		The companies have negligible investment needs as no assets are needed.

6. Outlook		
Trends in industry		<ul><li>Increase in mobile viewership</li><li>Increasing share of digital ads</li><li>Increasing acceptance off online fantasy leagues</li><li>Online social viewership increasing</li><li>Regional languages seeing great growth</li></ul>
Industry-specific risks		<ul><li>Retirement of star players</li><li>Fall in overall viewership of IPL</li><li>Advertisers moving to different platforms</li><li>Any government action stopping conduct of tournament</li><li>Match fixing, spot fixing issues etc.</li></ul>
Growth factors		<ul><li>Increase in advertising budget of companies</li><li>Regional language viewership</li><li>International viewership</li><li>Mobile viewership increasing watch hours</li></ul>
Variables for success in industry		<ul><li>Consistent performance by teams</li><li>Star 'hooks' in the team – MS Dhoni, Virat Kohli etc.</li><li>Online reputation management</li></ul>

Notes

Customer segmentation based on what the product would be used for

Viewers – Use it for entertainment

Advertisers – Use it for business growth

1. Customer profile – Viewers

Required gains

- Entertainment (Functional gain)

- Cheap; Not too expensive entertainment form (Functional gain)

- Sense of belonging (Social gain)

- Fan quotient for their teams (Psychological gain)

Desired gains

- Events around matches (Functional gain)

- Social viewership (Social gain)

- Exciting and competent matches (Psychological gains)

Unexpected Gains

- Gifts for watching the match (E.g. Hotstar contests) (Functional gain)

- Ad-free experiences (Functional gain)

- Access to behind the scenes of their teams (Psychological Gain)

Pains

- Too many ads

- Dull, one-sided matches

2. Customer profile – Advertisers

Required gains

- Brand building
- Customer awareness
- Increase sales

Desired gains

- Customer engagement
- Word of mouth
- Creation of 'buzz'
- Decent return on investment

Unexpected gains

- Viral effect of ads
- Exceptional ROI

Pains to be relieved

- A few platforms with very high reach
- Expensive ad rates
- Unpredictable ad results

Risks

- Create wrong positioning for the company
- Impact company's brand negatively
- Poor ROI from ad investments
- Industry value chain

3. Industry value chain

Infrastructure	ground, practice session management, equipment, ticket distribution partnerships
HRM	player management, support staff management, team bonding and building sessions
R&D	analytics for strategy, strategy for selection
Procurement	sponsorship procurement, ad agencies relationship management
Inbound logistics	
Operations	practice, match preparations, ticket management, accommodation arrangement, food and beverage arrangement
Outbound logistics	player logistics
Marketing and sales	media ads, events, TV shows for teams, social media management
Service	CSR

4. Industry map

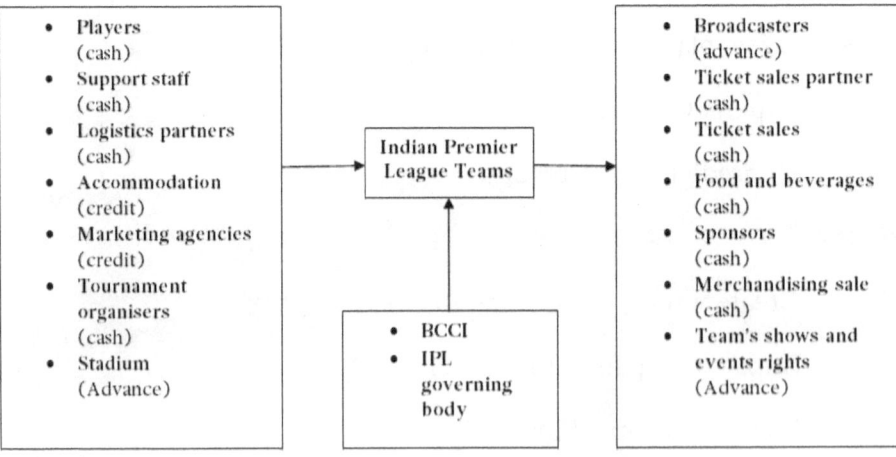

5. Demand (TV and digital)

- IPL over TV and digital has been on an upward trajectory throughout.

- IPL 12 had 462 million viewers watch the season. This is 12% y-o-y growth over the previous season.

- Advertisement realisation for broadcasters over TV is as follows:

  o 2014 – Rs 700 crore

  o 2015 – approx. Rs 1000 crore

  o 2016 – Rs 1200 crore

  o 2017 – Rs 1300 crore

  o 2018 – Rs 1750 crore

  o 2019 – Rs 2100 crore

- As a result, broadcast rights contract has also been on an upward trend over the years. This is the biggest part of revenue for teams.

6.

- In 2008, Sony acquired 10 years broadcast rights for Rs 8200 crore.

- In 2018, Star India acquired 5-year universal rights i.e., for 2018–22 for Rs 16,347 crore i.e. 2.55 billion USD, which translates to 500 million USD per year.

- Global media rights currently ($ per year):

  o NFL (American Football USA) -   6 billion USD

  o EPL (English football)   -   5 billion USD

- o   NBA (basketball USA)   –   2.66 billion USD

- o   MLB (baseball USA)   –   1.55 billion USD

- o   IPL (Indian cricket)   –   500 million USD

- • Ad realisations have been constantly increasing for broadcasters as seen in note 6.

- • Viewership is increasing with broadcast now in regional channels as well.

- • Next auction is due for 2023–27. That is when the franchisees will see the next increase in profits.

7. Teams like Kolkata Knight Riders, Mumbai Indians and Chennai Super Kings that have done well to attract slightly higher sponsor revenues than others. However, a major contribution comes from the central pool of revenues that is split equally among all competitor teams.

8. Different sports are organising leagues such as Pro Kabaddi for kabaddi, Hockey India League for hockey, and Indian Super League for football. These could take away some viewership from IPL. However, the viewership differential is very high. Yet, this can be a potential threat.

9. Supplier power: Players and support staff are considered as suppliers.

Number of suppliers in market	Many players
Availability of regular supply	Seasonal (only during IPL months)
Uniqueness of services	No substitute
Ability to substitute	No substitute
Switching costs	Effort
Dependency of industry on them	High dependency
Can the industry threaten to vertically integrate?	No

Importance of volume to supplier's profitability	No
Payment power with the supplier	Advance cash

10. Buyer power

Majorly advertisers are included as buyers.

Number of buyers/customers	Many
Size of buyers/ orders	A few medium-sized orders
How informed are the buyers	Very informed
Price sensitivity	Elastic
Demand-supply scenario	More demand
Can the buyers threaten vertical integration?	No
Payment power with buyers	Negligible credit

11. Threat of substitution

Availability of substitute to the goods	Distant substitutes available (other sports leagues)
Ability to substitute	Moderate
Cost of switching	Habit and preferences
Price performance of substitute vs the industry	Poor performance as preferred sport changes

12. Threat of entry

Time and cost of sizeable entry	Very high
Economics of scale	High economies of scale
Distribution strength required	High
Cost advantages to existing players	No
Switching costs for customers	Habit
Asset specificity in the industry	None
Proprietary product difference	Low
Network effect of the product	No

Protection against new entrants	Can only be introduced by IPL governing body
Brand identity	High
Reputation of existing firms	Reputation needed
Response by incumbents on new entry	No response

13. Competitive rivalry

Number of competitors in the industry	8 players
How concentrated is the industry	Concentrated
Differences in product quality	Homogenous
Cost of switching products	Habit and preferences
Is the industry growing?	Yes; growing industry
Overcapacity In the industry	No overcapacity
Fixed costs in the industry	Medium
Exit barriers in the industry	High
Basis of competition in the industry	Competition based on performance

14. Revenue break-up for each team in IPL

- Broadcasting rights (central pool)

  - Star India bought rights for global broadcasting and digital rights of IPL for Rs 16,347 crore for years 2018–22.

  - This translates to Rs 3200 crore per season.

  - BCCI retains 60% of it and distributes the remaining 40% equally to each team. Each team gets approximately Rs 160 crore each year from the central pool.

- Ticket sales, food and beverages

  - Teams earned Rs 30 crore - Rs 50 crore in 2018 for ticket sales, food and beverages during the home matches across the season.

- Team sponsorships

  - Teams earned Rs 30 crore – Rs 50 crore in 2018 from team sponsorships. These sponsors are different from tournament sponsors.

- Tournament prizes

  - IPL winner gets a prize of Rs 20 crore. There are prizes to be won by each team that finishes in the top 4.

- Team events broadcasting rights

  - Team events such as Inside CSK and Ami KKR also sell their broadcasting rights separately. However, not all teams do this.

15. **Expense break-up for each team in IPL**

- Player fee

  - Total player fee for each season is capped and increased slightly for each year. In 2019 IPL, each team spent Rs 82 crore for player fees.

- Support staff, logistics, team management, marketing and admin costs

  - Each team pays to their support staff, logistics, marketing and admin costs. These cost around Rs 40–50 crore.

- Franchise fees

  - Each team needs to pay franchise fees to BCCI each year. This is now fixed at 20% of the total revenues earned by the team during the year.

Industry Sheet

For Indian Express Logistics Industry

As on 31/10/2019

Factors	Note	Particulars
1. Value Proposition		
Customer segments	1	B2B, B2C, C2C
Customer gains	2,3,4	• Speed • Reliable • Single point of contact • Tracking facility available • Active customer support • Software integration with the company • Wide branch network • Low rates • Assurance that no parcels lost • Social impression of courier used
Customer pains	2,3,4	• Speed • Expensive • Not all pin codes covered • Unreliable • No cash-on-delivery facility • Lost shipments • No door-to-door service
Products and services	2,3,4	• Bulk transport (B2B) • Last mile delivery (B2C) • Parcel delivery(C2C) • Insured delivery

2. Activities and Participants		
Value chain	5	Key activities: • Fleet management • Warehouse management • Software management • Unloading and sorting • Distribution • Marketing and customer support • Branch network management
Industry map	6	Key players: • Fleet owners • Warehouse and distribution centre owners • Labour • B2B customers • B2C customers E.g. e-commerce sites
Demand-supply scenario	7	• Transportation demand is increasing y-o-y. Supply is flexible. • Warehousing space is currently in overdemand and undersupply state.
3. Industry Characteristics		
Market size study		Indian Express Logistics market size: • FY12 – Rs 10,870 crore • FY17 – Rs 22000 crore • FY22E – Rs 48000 crore
Industry stability		The industry mainly competes on price and reliability. Thus, there is not a very high pricing power. The volume drives profitability.

Pricing Power		It is a price-sensitive industry, with negligible pricing power. Those with established brands have a little pricing power.
Competitive life cycle		Growth stage • Industry growing fast • More players are adapting to express
Disruptions threat		None; sustaining innovation in technology involved
Regulations		• GST implementation • E-way bill • Multi-modal transport of goods act
4. Profit Forces		
Supplier power	8	Low
Buyer power	9	Moderate
Threat of substitution	10	Low
Threat of entry	11	High
Competitive rivalry in the industry	12	Moderate
5. Financial Health		
ROE and DuPont analysis		Moderate margin and turnover business; low leverage needed for asset-light models • ROE – attractive • ROA – attractive
Growth		Growth in teens in industry; slightly higher PAT growth due to operating leverage

Investment needs		Asset-heavy companies have a very high fixed capital and working capital investment needs. Asset-light model needs low investments.
6. Outlook		
Trends in industry		• Automation • Asset-light model • Modern warehouses • Multi-modal integration • 3PL business model • Data analytics
Industry-specific risks		• Too many pin codes without volume • Regulatory changes • Reputational risks • Network breakages • Lack of distribution network
Growth factors		• Economy growth • Growth of online businesses • GST allows lot of logistical improvements • Increase in 3PL and logistics outsourcing • Increase in value-added services
Variables for success in industry		• Volume • Network capabilities • Distribution strength

Notes

On the basis of 'who' the customer is – B2B, B2C and C2C

1. Customer profile – B2B customers

Required gains

- Trustworthy with the parcel
- Reliable delivery from source to destination

Desired gains

- Fast delivery
- Tracking facility available
- All pin codes covered
- Software integration
- Door-to-door service
- Single point of contact

Unexpected gains

- Insured delivery
- Social impression of the carrier used
- Active customer support

Pains to be relieved

- Slow delivery
- Time boundaries breached
- Damaged products during transit
- Expensive service
- No tracking facility available

2. Customer profile – B2C customers

Required gains

- Fast

- Software integration with the company

- Cash-on-delivery facility

Desired gains

- Insured

- Goods not damaged

- All pin codes covered

- Live tracking available

- Single point of contact

Unexpected gains

- Before-time delivery

- Social impression of the carrier used

- Active customer support

Pains to be relieved

- No tracking available

- Slow delivery

- Too expensive

- Not all pin codes covered

3. Customer Profile – C2C customers

Required gains

- Fast

- Reliable

- Cheap

Desired Gains

- Tracking facility available

- Active customer support

Unexpected Gains

- Insured delivery

Pains to be relieved

- No tracking available

- Lost packages

- Too expensive

- Industry value chain

4. Industry value chain

Infrastructure	logistics network maintenance, fleet maintenance, warehouse management, warehouse equipment management
HRM	drivers, warehouse workers, admin teams, tech teams
R&D	software management, data management, automation
Procurement	branch network, brokers for warehouse, brokers for fleet spot hire

Inbound logistics	unloading, sorting, labelling
Operations	sorting, palleting for those to be sorted, packaging, value-added services like knitting
Outbound logistics	sorting, fleet allocation, branch distribution
Marketing and sales	TV ads, sales representatives, branch network
Service	feedback, 24x7 helpline, live tracking, customer service representatives

5. Industry map

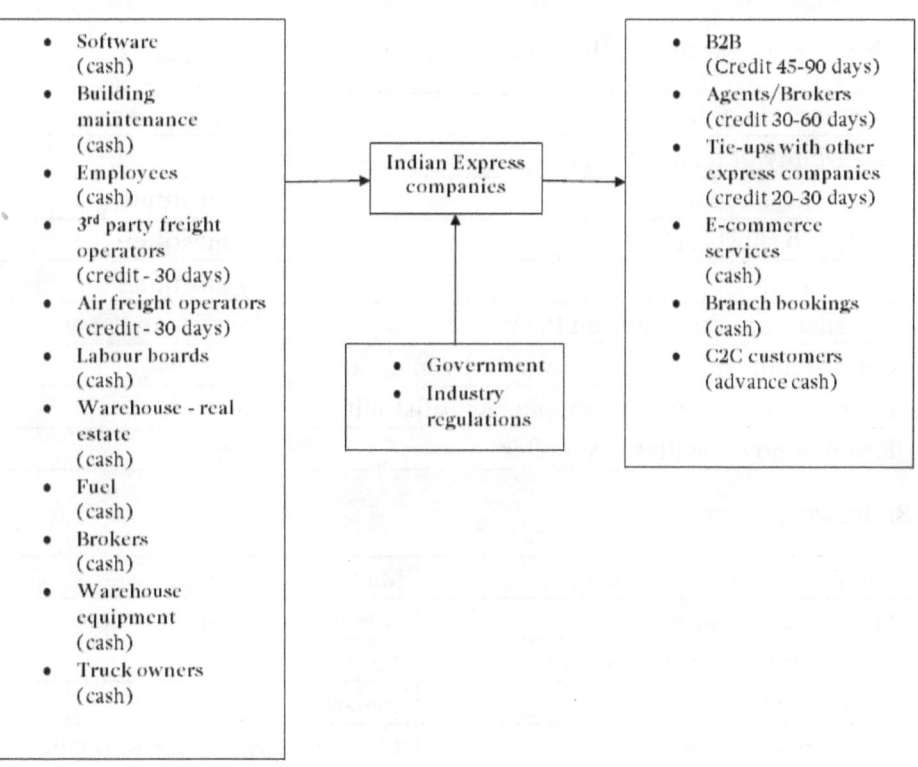

6. **Indian Express Logistics industry size:**

    - FY12 – Rs. 10,870 crore

    - FY17 – Rs. 22,000 crore

    - FY22E – Rs. 48000 crore

Supply in the industry is flexible. It does not take time for new capacity to enter and exit the industry. However, supply i.e. fleet ownership is very fragmented.

7. **Supplier power**

Labour, real estate and fleet owners are included in suppliers.

Number of suppliers in market	Many suppliers
Availability of regular supply	Easy
Uniqueness of services	No substitute
Ability to substitute	No substitute
Switching costs	No substitute
Dependency of industry on them	High dependency
Can the industry threaten to vertically integrate?	No
Importance of volume to supplier's profitability	Low
Payment power with the supplier	Cash

8. **Buyer power**

Number of buyers/customers	Many
Size of buyers/orders	A few medium-sized orders
How informed are the buyers	Very informed
Price sensitivity	Inelastic
Demand-supply scenario	More supply; but lack of quality supply
Can the buyers threaten vertical integration?	Yes
Payment power with buyers	Credit given: 15–30 days

9. Threat of substitution

Availability of substitute to the goods	No substitute
Ability to substitute	No substitute
Cost of switching	No substitute
Price performance of substitute vs the industry	No substitute

10. Threat of entry

Time and cost of sizeable entry	Moderate
Economics of scale	High economies of scale
Distribution strength required	High
Cost advantages to existing players	No
Switching costs for customers	Hassle, technology, dependency
Asset specificity in the industry	High asset specificity of owners
Proprietary product difference	Low
Network effect of the product	Yes
Protection against new entrants	No protection
Brand identity	High
Reputation of existing firms	Reputation needed
Response by incumbents on new entry	Moderate strategic response

11. Competitive rivalry

Number of competitors in the industry	A few competitors
How concentrated is the industry?	Moderately dilute
Differences in product quality	Minor differences in product
Cost of switching products	Hassle Dependency
Is the industry growing?	Yes; growing industry
Overcapacity in the industry	Seasonal overcapacity
Fixed costs in the industry	High fixed costs
Exit barriers in the industry	High
Basis of competition in the industry	Competition based on customer service and price

12. ROE and DuPont

TCI Express	2017	2018	2019
PAT margin	4.93%	6.55%	7.13%
Asset turnover	4.41x	3.56x	3.89x
Leverage	1.05	1.19	1.02
ROE	22.83%	27.75%	28.29%
ROA	36.4%	36.7%	45.2%
Dividend payout	16%	16%	16%
SGR	19.17%	23.31%	23.76%

Blue Dart	2015	2016	2017	2018	2019
PAT margin	5.67%	7.68%	5.21%	5.18%	2.84%
Asset turnover	6.21x	5.14x	4.81x	4.89x	4.46x
Leverage	1.18	1.30	1.30	1.07	1.23
ROE	41.54%	51.31%	32.57%	27.1%	15.57%
ROA	35.24%	39.5%	25.04%	25.34%	12.60%
Dividend payout	294%	36%	25%	21%	33%
SGR		32.84%	24.42%	21.4%	10.27%

(The company undertook a massive network expansion plan in the last few years to cover all pin codes across India. That affects profitability in the medium term, as volume takes time to build over these routes.)

13. PAT and revenue growth

TCI Express	2017	2018	2019
Revenue growth		18%	15.7%
PAT growth		56%	25.8%

Blue Dart	2015	2016	2017	2018	2019
Revenue growth	17.29%	12.8%	4.9%	4.05%	13.4%
PAT growth	4.8%	52.7%	-29%	3.5%	-38.1%

14. Investment needs

TCI Express	2017	2018	2019
CFO	52	74	78
Fixed investment	38	62	19
FCF	14	8	59
Revenue	750	885	1024

Blue Dart	2015	2016	2017	2018	2019
CFO	153	361	225	317	243
Fixed investment	44	119	123	199	287
FCF	109	242	102	118	(44)
Revenue	2272	2563	2690	2799	3174

15. Major practices in Indian Express Logistics industry

- Renting the warehouses instead of ownership

- Owning the warehouse equipment, designed in-house

- Owning small part of the fleet, outsourcing the rest

- Asset-light model to scale

- Asset-heavy model to consolidate

- Focus on multi-modal network creation

- Collaborations with small players

16. History of express logistics worldwide

- The first serious logistics attempts were made during the supply of food and wartime material. The supplies were carried on animal backs and became critical factors behind winning and losing wars. Since then, logistics has slowly and steadily evolved till the internet age, where virtual presence of companies needs them to be prompt in delivery.

- Railroads, steam engines, ships, automobiles followed by planes came to change the face of the logistics industry and started companies that we see today.

- As newer and newer modes of transport came, industries became larger and communication became easier, companies could grow to scale unimagined before.

- In the modern age, companies like Fedex, UPS, Nippon Express and DHL went on to become world leaders.

- Most of these companies started early in their countries. As industrial revolution caught up, they grew, achieving economies of scale. Once they had scale, they could pick and choose new markets and they began to dominate the markets over time.

- Those who could not achieve economies of scale failed.

- DHL started as a small company in the US and was bought by Deutsche Post group. Once it was bought, it gained scale merits and access to Deutsche Post's network system. So, it succeeded in capitalising on its scale and opportunity, using mergers and acquisitions.

- Nippon Express was started in 1872. It was mainly used for wartime material and personal transport. That is where it got access to early-scale advantages.

- XPO, STO, SF Express and YTO are Chinese companies that grew with the support of Alibaba as China e-commerce took off.

- Fedex began in 1971 and pioneered live tracking of packages, which instantly got it volumes. It capitalised on it using M&A to gain scale benefits.

- The products and customers for such companies have changed a lot. From delivering majorly large parcels, they now have to deal with small shipments for retail customers.

- The customer needs a quick, accessible and reliant logistics provider.

- The government has been supportive towards the industry.

- The biggest challenge to the industry has been high operating leverage, high fleet and personal management.

Further Reading

For those inclined towards reading more, here is a list of books that shall serve great to benefit the readers. These books would add great value to the readers who wish to make a career or already have one in investing. All these books have been written by prolific researchers or investors who are very well established in their art.

- Value Proposition Design: *How to Create Products and Services Customers Want* (Strategyzer) by Alexander Osterwald, Yves Pigneur, Gregory Bernarda and Alan Smith

- Business Model Generation: *A Handbook for Visionaries, Game Changers, and Challengers* (Strategyzer) by Alexander Osterwald and Yves Pigneur

- *The Competitive Strategy: Techniques for Analysing Industries and Competitors* by Michael E. Porter

- Competitive Advantage: *Creating and Sustaining Superior Performance* by Michael E. Porter

- The Little Book That Builds Wealth: *The Knockout Formula for Finding Great Investments* (Little Books. Big Profits)

- Research paper - "Measuring the Moat" published by Credit Suisse in 2013, written by Michael Mauboussin

- Zero to One: *Note on Startups, or How to Build the Future* by Peter Thiel

- Value Migration: *How to Think Several Moves Ahead of the Competition (Management of Innovation and Change)* by Adrian J. Slywotzky

- HBR's 10 Must Reads: *On Strategy (Harvard Business Review Must Reads)* by HBR

- The Five Rules for Successful Stock Investing: *Morningstar's Guide to Building Wealth and Winning in the Market*

- Competition Demystified: *A Radically Simplified Approach to Business Strategy* by Bruce C. Greenwald and Judd Kahn

- *Berkshire Hathway Annual Letters* by Warren E. Buffet

Also, the next book in the series — *Big Fish – The Complete Guide to Identifying Winner Companies in Any Industry* and the third book on management sheets shall be published in the coming time.

Also, a course shall be updated about the "Qualitatives" on ZebraLearn website around December of 2020 or earlier.

Please write to me at anuragsunderka@gmail.com to get in touch and discuss any topic regarding the book. I would love to hear from you.

Happy Reading!

Before You End

The idea of this book as already mentioned is to provide an exhaustive and most importantly, an 'implementable' guide for those in the investing industry or are looking to get into it. The focus of the work at each step has been to make the work as exhaustive as possible and as applicable as possible. This, however, was not possible by ignoring the wonderful work done by others in the field in the past. Many ideas discussed in the book that make sure the process and 'Industry Sheet' is exhaustive have been either borrowed or inspired by past works in the field. I did not feel fit to leave out such amazing work, as it would have defied the entire purpose – Exhaustivity and Applicability for the reader. I have taken these ideas sitting in rich libraries and tried making them more applicable for the reader. The inclusion of these ideas make sure that now the 'Industry Sheets' is exhaustive and applicable. Here, I include a list of sources.

1. Value Proposition Model – Has been inspired by the book *Value Proposition Design* by Alex Osterwalder and his team. I do not completely agree with the customer profile side of their model and have made changes accordingly in mine.

2. Value Chain – It was first introduced in the book *Competitive Advantage* by Michael E. Porter.

3. Industry Map – It was first discussed by Michael Mauboussin.

4. Profit Pool – First introduced by two researchers at Bain & Co.

5. Five Forces model – This iconic piece of work was introduced in the book *Competitive Strategy* by Michael E. Porter.

6. Disruptions – The ideas have been discussed by Harvard Business School Professor Clayton Christensen in his books and research papers over the years.

In no way do I claim these to be my pieces of work. I have mentioned all the sources in the text, wherever it is applicable. These have been a result of countless hours of effort put in by the researchers and their team, and they are the ones who deserve complete credit for it. I would also insist that the reader checks out the researchers' complete work as well.

Also, many examples included in the book, were not searched for the purpose of being included here initially but were created over past few years as routine investment related research. It is not possible to create a list of all the sources referred to over time. The primary sources are – Corporate communications by the companies, interviews of management, coverage by media companies, Government data, publicly shared data by other financial firms and few others. Credit is due to each of them.

In case you want to discuss anything about the book, please reach me at my email address – anuragsunderka@gmail.com

Reader's Handbook: How to Create Industry Sheets with Indian Logistics Sector in Focus

Steps to use the QR code to access the Reader's Handbook:

1. Open any QR code scanner app that you may be using or else go to website – qrcodescan.in (Preferably using mobile)

2. Allow permission to access camera.

3. Scan the Code above using the camera and you will get the link to access the file. Download the file.

References

1. https://www.entrepreneur.com/article/317725

2. https://www.psychologytoday.com/us/blog/the-athletes-way/201403/the-neuroscience-social-pain

3. http://aronkiptarus.blogspot.com/2012/10/the-value-chain.html

4. https://www.lucidchart.com/blog/what-is-value-chain-analysis

5. https://mpra.ub.uni-muenchen.de/66799/8/MPRA_paper_66799.pdf

6. http://analystreports.som.yale.edu/internal/F2013/MJ/Measuring%20the%20Moat.pdf

7. http://documents.mx/documents/profit-pools.html

8. https://www.daytrading.com/commodity-cycle

9. https://blog.arkieva.com/demand-forecasting/

10. http://www.strategystreet.com/blog/causes_and_symptoms_of_overcapacity

11. https://en.wikipedia.org/wiki/Capacity_planning

12. https://www.slideshare.net/aju721/cadbury-6110613

13. https://www.investopedia.com/terms/p/pricingpower.asp

14. https://www.icsi.edu/media/website/Business%20 Economics%20(FndProg).pdf

15. https://corporatefinanceinstitute.com/resources/knowledge/ strategy/industry-life-cycle/

16. https://www.slideshare.net/ashishKPD/product-life-cycle-26664029

17. http://www.ialc.org/file/documents/workshops/2015-rouen/ Industry_lifecycle_seminar_handout.pdf

18. https://www.encyclopedia.com/entrepreneurs/encyclopedias-almanacs-transcripts-and-maps/industry-life-cycle

19. https://corporatefinanceinstitute.com/resources/knowledge/ strategy/industry-life-cycle/

20. https://pt.scribd.com/document/67260150/stm

21. https://www.forbes.com/sites/carolinehoward/2013/03/27/ you-say-innovator-i-say-disruptor-whats-the-difference/?utm_ campaign=forbestwittersf&utm_medium=socia&utm_ source=twitter

22. https://hbr.org/sponsored/2019/04/7-disruptive-forces-that-leaders-should-incorporate-into-growth-strategies

23. https://www.hbs.edu/forum-for-growth-and-innovation/blog/ post/confronting-a-new-market-disruption-disruptor

24. https://medium.com/@tom_bartman/confronting-a-new-market-disruption-when-disrupting-the-disruptor-is-the-only-way-to-succeed-f02355ad919b

25. https://sites.google.com/site/bus141abrahamruizwikipage/mis-and-you/week-4

26. https://medium.com/@imnotjk/the-end-of-disruption-ab11fffa34fd

27. https://preferredpayments.com/importance-being-know-industry-news/

28. https://yourfreetemplates.com/porters-five-forces-template/

29. https://www.nhm.ac.uk/discover/what-is-natural-selection.html

30. https://www.historians.org/about-aha-and-membership/aha-history-and-archives/historical-archives/why-study-history-(1998)

31. http://www.jfklancer.com/Education.html

32. https://judithcurry.com/2013/07/29/uncertainty-lost-in-translation/

Author Bio

Anurag is a business researcher, who has over the last four years developed a business research model titled '9-Point Business Circuit'. He has also developed the concept of 'Qualitatives', which includes 'Industry Sheet', 'Business Sheet' and 'Management Sheet' and a financial analysis framework.

Anurag has cleared all levels of the CFA exam. He is a pass out of the Finnacle Investment Academy. He is a business researcher and an entrepreneur. He is also a co-founder of ZebraLearn and ZebraPro. ZebraLearn focuses on education and research in the financial domain and ZebraPro focuses on developing an AI-powered workstation for investors and analysts.

www.ingramcontent.com/pod-product-compliance
Lightning Source LLC
Chambersburg PA
CBHW020858180526
45163CB00007B/2544